Suffering the Truth

Occasional Sermons and Reflections

Suffering the Truth

Occasional Sermons and Reflections

Chris K. Huebner

CMU Press
Winnipeg, Manitoba
2020

CMU Press
500 Shaftesbury Blvd
Winnipeg, Manitoba
R3P 2N2
www.cmu.ca/cmupress

Layout: Gordon Zerbe
Cover Design: Matt Veith

Printed in Canada
by Art Bookbindery, Winnipeg, Manitoba

Library and Archives Canada Cataloguing in Publication

Title: Suffering the truth : occasional sermons and reflections / Chris K. Huebner.
Names: Huebner, Chris K., 1969- author.
Identifiers: Canadiana 2019022374X | ISBN 9781987986075 (softcover)
Subjects: LCSH: Mennonites—Sermons. | CSH: Sermons, Canadian (English)
Classification: LCC BX8127.H85 S94 2019 | DDC 252/.097—dc23

For John, Jeff, Isaac, and Carrie

Table of Contents

Acknowledgements

My thanks go out, first of all, to the worshipping communities who were originally on the receiving end of these efforts. Writing and speaking are always, to a certain extent, occasioned by specific audiences and contexts. In the Christian tradition, this relationship is customarily developed by invoking images of food and nourishment. It was common to speak of the sermon as an offering of food that is given in the hope that it might provide the right sort of nutritional value for the audience that receives it. Since sermons assume a different audience than the genre of academic writing to which I am more accustomed, I am all too aware of the danger of offering the wrong sort of food, or perhaps the right food that may have been prepared in the wrong way. To those for whom these sermons and reflections were "too academic," I apologize for delivering what might come across as bigger than bite sized chunks that were perhaps a bit undercooked and therefore somewhat difficult to digest. I can only hope that the congregations who heard these sermons when they were originally delivered were left with something of nutritional value once they were sufficiently chewed over.

Two communities, in particular, deserve special recognition for the way they have cultivated environments that are open to hearing from lay preachers who are given the occasional opportunity to speak. My home congregation of Charleswood Mennonite Church in Winnipeg has no shortage of fine preachers. Because of this, it can be an intimidating place to deliver a sermon. But at the same time, one can always be confident that even if things go slightly awry, someone else will take to the pulpit and get them back on track before too long. At Canadian Mennonite University, where I have taught for almost twenty years, the community gathers for worship twice a week. I suspect I am not the only one who has at times imagined CMU chapel as a sort of experimental preaching lab. The freedom to try out ideas and approaches that might not be considered the wisest of choices in other contexts, not to mention a wide range of faculty, students, and guests who have a good sense of what to do with that freedom, has nourished a vibrant and varied worship experience that I have really grown to appreciate over the years.

Although they are quite different in several notable respects, these two communities have one thing in common. They are the only ones that have invited me to preach more than once. I suspect that this should be interpreted less as a sign of what they think of my preaching and more as an indication of the fact that they are stuck with me. Either way, I am endlessly grateful that I am able to call them home.

I am fortunate to have received spiritual nourishment from a number of preachers who embody the characteristics of good preaching. At Charleswood, John Braun served as my pastor for over twenty years. His ability to bring to life the biblical story and his reflections on the Christian tradition's efforts to embrace it faithfully in a variety of different contexts have left a lasting mark on our congregation. I will miss him and wish him all the best as he no doubt enjoys preaching less frequently in his retirement. More recently, Jeff Friesen has challenged the Charleswood community to consider what it looks like to live faithfully in the specific context of the city of Winnipeg, particularly in light of the fact that it continues to bear the marks of fractured relationships between settler and indigenous peoples. It was an honor to have been asked to preach at Jeff's ordination service and I am happy to include the sermon delivered on that occasion in this collection. Isaac Villegas of Chapel Hill Mennonite Fellowship in Chapel Hill, North Carolina exemplifies an uncommon mix of incisive intellectual precision and gentle charity that defies all stereotypes about what a pastor is commonly thought to look like. In addition to thanking him for his pastoral leadership, I must also thank Isaac for the gift of his friendship and the rich conversations that were possible when we had the opportunity to spend regular time together during a sabbatical leave spent in Durham in 2008-09. More recently, and regrettably all too briefly, I had the good fortune of worshipping with Carrie Ballenger at the Lutheran Church of the Redeemer in the heart of Jerusalem's Old City. This unusual congregation, where church members are defined as "those who attend more than once" and who are at any rate typically outnumbered on Sunday mornings by visitors from around the world, is gifted each week by Carrie's lively stories and moving reflections that nourish and sustain the kind of hope that is all too rare in the divided world of contemporary Jerusalem and its surrounding area. In different ways, these four pastors model the forms of preaching to which I aspire on the rare occasions when I am invited to do the work they so admirably perform on a regular basis. As a small token of thanks for the gift of their profound witness, I dedicate this book to them.

Finally, a word of thanks to CMU Press for taking on this project. In particular, I am grateful to Paul Doerksen for helping me to conceive the idea of the book in the first place and to Gordon Zerbe for seeing it through to publication.

Publication of this book was made possible with the support of a CMU Faculty Research Grant.

An earlier version of Chapter 1 was originally published as Chris K. Huebner, "Advent and Idolatry: A Sermon," *Vision: A Journal for Church and Theology* 12:1 (Spring 2011): 77-82.

An earlier version of Chapter 10 was originally published in Chris K. Huebner, *A Precarious Peace: Yoderian Explorations on Theology, Knowledge, and Identity*. Scottdale, PA: Herald Press, 2006.

Introduction

On Preaching as Preening,
or the Difficulty of Preaching Occasionally

In canto XXIX, near the end of the *Paradiso* and indeed the entire *Divine Comedy*, Dante unleashes a searing rant against bad preaching. He places his invective in the mouth of Beatrice, who serves as the spokesperson for much of the theological reflection offered in *Paradiso*. In this particular scene, Beatrice is addressing Dante, who is nearing the end of the course of theological education he undergoes in his journey through the celestial spheres. This pilgrimage through the light of the stars that constitute the heavens began in a much darker place. Dante's epic theological poem opens in the middle of a forest where he found himself lost and entirely alone, separated not only from God but from any other human beings. But now, as Dante and Beatrice approach the very home in which God resides along with the angels and the blessed saints in a state of enduring friendship, Beatrice rails against preachers who "ply their trade with buffoonery and jokes."[1] These preachers can be identified, she suggests, by their swollen egos which expand a little bit more with each burst of laughter they manage to elicit from the crowd they are addressing. The translator Robert Hollander describes their efforts as a form of "preaching as preening."[2] Beatrice is critical of sermons that are presented as if they are offerings in a contest among orators who are engaged in a battle against one another to win the approval of an audience that asks for nothing more than to be entertained. If she had been speaking in the 21st century rather than the 14th, Beatrice may well have referred to the significance given to television ratings or to examples drawn from reality television shows in which the votes of viewers determine the outcome of the story. In

---

[1] Dante, *Paradiso*, XXIX, 115 (p. 793). Subsequent references to the poem will be made parenthetically in the body of the text.
[2] Ibid., 805.

Dante's time as in our own, the church finds itself in a complicated relationship with the entertainment industry.

Beatrice is concerned that both the preachers and their congregations have become captivated by the "love of show" (XXIX, 86) in a way that suggests they have lost sight of God. Describing the preachers, she says that "Each strives to gain attention by inventing new ideas. . .but the Gospel remains silent." (XXIX, 94-96) Indeed, she suggests that the silence of the Gospel is proportional to the volume of the shouting that issues from the pulpit. (XXIX, 105) This is not preaching the truth of God, she warns, but rather the proliferation of lies. By gunning for laughs and other forms of approval, preachers who are called to tend to the well-being of their flocks actually end up leaving their congregations fundamentally malnourished. Their preoccupation with entertainment serves to create an "ignorant flock" that is "fed on wind" rather than the nurturing spiritual truth of the Gospel. (XXIX, 106-107)

Beatrice makes clear, however, that the blame does not rest solely on the shoulders of the preachers who struggle to shepherd their congregations. The sheep under their care also experience the piercing sting of her sharp tongue. The congregation is equally part of the problem in the eyes of Beatrice because they have equated the word of God with something that leaves them amused and self-satisfied. Beatrice thus elaborates a scene in which preachers and their congregations are entangled in a vicious cycle that leaves them all "estranged from truth."[3] Not only are they estranged from the truth, they are equally estranged from one another. Each of them, in their own way, desires nothing more than the satisfaction of the self. This creates conditions that serve to block them from being drawn into the strange and excessively generous love of God. Beatrice seems to be suggesting that to be preoccupied with entertainment is to be preoccupied with self-confirming loves that underwrite an invulnerable posture of mastery.

Is this to suggest that one who participates in the giving and receiving of laughter is necessarily implicated in an irredeemably corrupted form of exchange? Is Beatrice claiming that a good preacher is one who delivers excruciatingly boring sermons? Does her critique of preaching as preening assume a formula that measures the truth of our speech about God as though it is inversely proportional to the amount

---

[3] Ibid., 807.

of enjoyment it elicits? Does she mean that the better a sermon is, the less it will be appreciated by those who hear it? More generally, is she calling for the church to develop austere and exceedingly dour forms of worship? If one is at all familiar with the details of Dante's journey, it should be clear that the answer to all of these questions is a resounding no.

We might begin to understand how he provides such an answer if we can appreciate that in Beatrice's rant against bad preaching, as in so many other scenes in the *Divine Comedy*, there is an echo of the forest scene with which the story began some 95 cantos earlier. There, Dante remained stuck in the darkness of the forest because he was seeking to achieve a sort of intellectual transcendence that is capable of apprehending the good by relying entirely on his own merits. Call it the path of intellectual assent. The love he thought he had for Beatrice was equally flawed because he approached it as a possession he could work to achieve. In both of these ways—one rational and the other emotional—Dante exhibits a kind of blindness because he looks at the world with eyes that are fundamentally flawed. On the one hand, they look straight ahead or aim upward in a linear fashion. On the other hand, they are turned back on themselves in a way that suggests a spirit of self-confirmation. In both cases, Dante refers to these as eyes that are "fixed." Theirs is a static vision. By the time he reaches the scene of Beatrice's sermon on bad preaching, Dante has been schooled, first by Virgil and then by Beatrice herself, in a new kind of vision. We might describe it as a refracted or triangulated vision that is mediated by the divine gift of God's grace. Dante learns, for example, that he can only truly see Beatrice when he learns to see her as the spiritual being she is when she is seen by God. It is important to recognize that this new way of seeing does not involve coming to see a new range of objects. Rather, he is learning to see with eyes that have been theologically disciplined. Without getting into too much detail, we might note that this is a form of vision that has been trained by the theological virtues of faith, hope, and charity. Dante places this lesson in the mouths of some nymphs who pay him a visit during his encounter with Beatrice in earthly paradise, atop the mountain of Purgatory:

'Here we are nymphs and in heaven we are stars;
before Beatrice descended to the world
we were ordained to serve as her handmaids.

We will bring you to her eyes. But to receive
the joyous light they hold, the other three
    [i.e., the theological virtues],
who look much deeper into things, shall sharpen yours.'[4]

One of the key roles that Beatrice plays for Dante is to help him keep his eyes properly disciplined. When he gives in to temptation and stares at her directly with a possessive gaze that sees her as the "pretty girl from Florence"[5] she cries out, admonishing him that his eyes are "too fixed!" (*Purgatorio* XXXII, 9) Beatrice thus functions to refashion Dante's gaze and reorder his love in such a way that they seek not a possession to be grasped but to approach the world through what we might call a logic or grammar of gift. This is not a rejection of love, laughter, and the world as such. Rather, it is a dispossessive way of seeing and being in the world which recognizes that it is not ours to control.

In order to spell this out, we do well to recall that Dante's project in the *Divine Comedy* is an attempt to reimagine the very nature of his own task as a poet. Whereas he had earlier approached poetry as an attempt to entertain with fabulous images that win praise for the poet, Dante now comes to see poetry as a sort of self-sacrifice, a mystical erasure of the ego. He wants to do something new with poetry by reconceiving it as a thoroughly theological enterprise. The Dante scholar, John Freccero, calls it the "poetics of conversion."[6] Christian Moevs helpfully summarizes the vision of Dante's new poetry as follows: "there is no path to understanding, happiness, or immortality that does not go through self-sacrifice, through the death to blind self-interest that is an awakening to love, to freedom, to the infinite in and as the finite: to Christ."[7] Dante's poetics of conversion can be contrasted with the "heroic" approach he ascribes to Ulysses a few cantos earlier in *Paradiso* XXVII. To quote Moevs once again:

Ulysses sought understanding by 'becoming a knower of the world,' seeking to devour the world in the few days left to his senses, without sacrificing his own ego or sense of self; he pursues the sun in a voyage governed by the ephemeral light reflected by the moon, the light of finite created intelligence, which waxes and wanes five

---

[4] Dante, *Purgatorio*, XXXI, 106-111 (p. 699). Subsequent references to the poem will be made parenthetically in the body of the text.

[5] Ibid., 726.

[6] See Freccero, *Dante: The Poetics of Conversion*, 1-28.

[7] Moevs, *The Metaphysics of Dante's* Comedy, 171.

times, corresponding perhaps to the senses. Ulysses is presumptuous not for *what* he sought—deification, in Dante's world, is the true goal of every human being—but for *how* he sought it: without turning within to know himself, without sacrificing his unquestioned identification with, and reliance on, a finite mind and body, without surrendering to the ground of his own being.[8]

All of this suggests that we should understand the task of the preacher as Beatrice presents it as analogous to the task of the poet as Dante presents it throughout the *Comedy* as a whole. Even as he sets out on a revolutionary path to create a radically theological epic, it is important to appreciate that Dante remains very much a poet. His poetic work may come to resemble that of a preacher, but he also seeks to remain an entertainer of sorts. In other words, Dante believes his poetry is something to be enjoyed by others. In describing his new poetry, he emphasizes that there is a sweetness to it. The name he gives to it is "dolce still novo," the sweet new style. (*Purgatorio* XXIV, 57)

So the contrast Beatrice is drawing when she excoriates bad preachers and their congregations is not a contrast between something that is pleasurable and something that is painful, as the questions above might lead us to suspect. We miss the point she is making if we treat it as a question of the presence or absence of laughter or entertainment as such. On the contrary, Dante insists that we are right to enjoy his new poetry, perhaps even to smile or laugh when we hear it. But if the poetry works, it will elicit a new sort of laughter. If there is laughter here, in other words, it might be called the laughter of God. This is a laughter that serves to surrender the finite mind and ego rather than strengthening them.[9] It corrects the egocentric laughter that arises when we take ourselves too seriously. It is the delicate balance of this task that Beatrice is underscoring in her comments on the art of preaching. Like Dante's "higher" poetry, the preacher seeks not to win approval but to speak truthfully of God. This only happens if the preacher herself fades from view and the congregation ceases to be blindly self-absorbed.

It is important to take note of the setting for Beatrice's reflections on preaching. This scene takes place in the Crystalline Sphere, the ninth and uppermost part of the created heavens. This is the highest point of God's creation in time. It is from here that the temporal character which defines the rest of the created order has its beginning. Beyond the

---

[8] Ibid., 133.
[9] I owe this way of putting it to Moevs, 91.

Crystalline sphere lies the Empyrean—the uncreated, eternal, and placeless place in which God resides along with the angels and saints. That a discussion of preaching is located here speaks to the lofty nature of its task. But it is equally important to appreciate this scene is not located in the Empyrean itself. Like the virtues of faith and hope, preaching is not necessary when we are in the very presence of God. So it is fair to say that there will no preaching in heaven, an observation that is sure to delight restless children who struggle to sit through sermons. Rather, preaching is an earthly task. It is an essentially human activity. Though it speaks of the Creator, it does so in a manner of speech that is appropriate for creatures. Preaching is necessary, in other words, precisely because we are not divine. Among other things, it sets out to save us from the temptation to think and act as if we occupy the place of God. But this is what both the preacher and the congregation seem to have forgotten in Beatrice's depiction of bad preaching. They can both be said to exhibit a posture of invulnerability. But this is to enact a sort of self-deception that is forgetful of its very creatureliness. That is because to be a creature is to be a being whose life is essentially fragile, dependent, and vulnerable.

It will no doubt seem odd to some that I have appealed to a late medieval Catholic figure like Dante in order to introduce a collection of sermons that were delivered in Mennonite settings. Is this not the sort of approach that the people who came to be known as Mennonites sought to leave behind during the tumultuous years of the early 16th century? I will leave it to others to settle that complex question. But at the same time, it bears stating that the richness of the Christian tradition is surely obscured if we seek to eliminate its constitutive oddness. One of the great gifts of Dante is his ability to capture the complicated nature of the theological task in a way that avoids reducing it to a series of "positions."

At any rate, I begin with these reflections on Dante because they help to capture the sense of terror I experience every time I am invited to preach. Beatrice's comments on preaching sound a sobering note of caution, perhaps even of outright danger, for anyone who dares to step up to the pulpit to deliver a sermon. They are a reminder that preaching is a demanding and inherently difficult task and properly so. There may be some who are rightly described as natural preachers. But I am fairly certain that I am not one of them. Preaching most definitely does not come naturally to me. Although I have the utmost admiration for those who are called to preach on a regular basis, this is not something I ever set out to do even on an occasional basis, let alone a more regular one. It is perhaps for this reason that I have only ever found myself preaching when I have been invited by others to do so. And to be honest, I am thankful that I am not asked very often, because I find it a challenging and emotionally draining task. But despite its difficulty, I have come to appreciate the hard work it involves. That others have found themselves in a position of thinking it might be a good idea to have me deliver a sermon, and sometimes even to do so again, must surely be a sign that that God has a robust sense of humour. Nevertheless, when I am occasionally invited to preach, I find it helpful to be mindful of Beatrice's harsh words on preaching and Dante's more general understanding of the difficulty of speaking truthfully of God.

The fact that we may identify some as natural preachers does not contradict the fact that preaching is not a natural activity. What we call natural preachers, then, are those who have been given the gift of doing what comes unnaturally. The very character of the Christian life turns upon the acknowledgment that we are somehow at odds with some forms of our natural existence, such as our desire for self-preservation. This is why baptism is said to mark the beginning of a new life. And preaching is a sort of commentary on the nature and implications of that new life. The sermon might be said to offer what the philosopher Stanley Cavell calls a "scene of instruction."[10] It sets out to paint scenes that describe what that new life might look like. It strives to make connections between aspects of that new life that might otherwise be obscured by our disposition to avoid the strangeness of life. In this respect, we might say, with Cavell again, that theology is "always something to be dispersed." Good preaching, then, might be described as a way of "speaking beyond oneself." The sermon is "the place where you talk about all the things you can't talk about."[11] In doing so, it offers

---

[10] See Dula, *Cavell, Companionship, and Christian Theology*, 57-74. I had always intended to include this reference to Cavell as a way of describing how I understand the work of the sermon. It is all the more poignant that I type these words on June 20, 2018, the day after he passed away.

[11] Cavell offered these words in a response to a question posed by my friend Peter Dula in a seminar discussion that followed a lecture Cavell gave at Duke University on October 12, 2009. The lecture was based on his memoir, *Little Did I Know: Excerpts from Memory* (Stanford: Stanford University Press, 2010). The exchange can be heard at around the 41-minute mark of the following video recording of that seminar: https://www.youtube.com/watch?v=DHswwGefmw8. I

a kind of grammatical instruction so that we might be positioned better to speak truthfully about the strange new life into which we have been called by God.

I have been speaking about Beatrice's harsh words regarding the giving and receiving of sermons. It would be a mistake, however, to suggest that she sets out only to castigate and scold. We should also be able to identify a sense of consolation in her comments on the nature of preaching. Though her words may well scare us, they should also be heard as words that welcome us into the risky business of preaching. There is a sense in which all preaching is destined to be bad preaching. Or at least there will always be something about it that is destined to be less than entirely good. Preaching, in other words, will always involve an element of preening. That is because sermons are delivered and heard by humans and not angels. A sermon certainly cannot be good if by that we take it to mean that it has somehow uttered the last word on a given topic. Theology is a discourse that does not seek to utter the last word. It does not strive to bring discussions to a close, but rather seeks to keep the unending task of receiving the creative gifts of God going in a meaningful way. If anything, we might interpret Beatrice to be saying that a sermon should aim high because its goal is to say something meaningful of the life into which we have been called by God. But at the same time, we should also acknowledge that we will fail. Moreover, if she suggests that it is right to fail, she also reminds us that we will not be defined by our failures.

Perhaps the key lesson of Beatrice and Dante is that good preaching is that which arises from a robust appreciation of one's essential fragility. Call it a posture of homiletic vulnerability. Ours is not the pristine speech of angels, but the faltering and stammering words of wounded animals. In recognizing this, we might even find that there is a certain lightness to the task of preaching. It is a lightness and freedom that arises when we realize it is not up to us to ensure that everything comes out right. One of the most important lessons I learned from Stanley Hauerwas is that theology only works, if it can be said to work at all, when it does not arise from a sense of desperation. Theologians and preachers go wrong, Hauerwas suggests, when they seek to make the words they must use necessary. In a way that echoes the words of

---

owe Peter a sincere word of thanks for being patient with me while I slowly came to appreciate how right he was about the importance of Cavell for what I take the work of theology to be.

8

Beatrice, he observes that the result of this false assumption is usually a form of "desperate shouting."[12] Good preaching, then, is preaching that does not arise from a sense of desperation. It does not set out to supply all the answers or even to identify the right questions. Rather, it seeks to say something that might help to cultivate a posture of receptivity to the overflowing goodness of God.

I have subtitled this book in a way that acknowledges the extent to which my preaching can be described as occasional. This is so in at least three different but interrelated ways. First, I have already alluded to the fact that I only find myself at the pulpit every once in a while, at most once or twice a year. Second, it is also worth noting that these sermons and reflections only exist at all because they were occasioned by others. Preaching is not always offered as a response to a specific invitation of some sort. But it is nevertheless the case that all of my preaching has been. By saying this, I do not mean to disavow the words that constitute this book, let alone to lay the groundwork for placing the blame on others where they might be said to go wrong. But it is surely significant that they do not arise out of any sort of formal office of preaching.

There is also a third sense in which these sermons can be described as occasional. That is because they happen to coincide with special occasions that celebrate key moments in the Christian calendar. Indeed, many of them fall on days that would in other traditions be called feast days. Because of this, I have decided to order them according to the liturgical calendar. So the book begins with a sermon on Advent, which celebrates the beginning of the Christian year. It moves through the seasons of Epiphany, Lent, and Easter. And it concludes with a sermon that was delivered on Peace Sunday, which is observed by many Mennonite churches mid-November, just before a new year once again commences with Advent.

At the same time, the book also includes reflections on other moments and themes that might be said to speak of those times that fall in between the special feast days. These are grouped together in one of two periods that are traditionally called Ordinary Time. The first such period celebrates Christ's earthly ministry. Here, I have included two sermons that reflect on the perplexity of our relation to Jesus and the very task of ministry, along with a faith story that reflects on my own perplexity with the experience of growing up in Jerusalem. The second

---

[12] Hauerwas, *Working with Words: On Learning to Speak Christian* (Eugene, OR: Cascade Books, 2011), xi.

period of Ordinary Time anticipates the coming kingdom of God. Since the kingdom of God is characterized by the ceaseless enjoyment of perfect love, here I have included three celebratory reflections on love: two were originally delivered in the context of university graduation exercises and the third was a tribute to my parents in honor of their 50th wedding anniversary. Though each of these sermons and reflections stands alone, the book as a whole can be said to offer in some small way an account of the way the Christian life is given shape by the liturgical rhythm of the Christian year.

In closing, I want to emphasize the sense in which the occasional refers to something irregular. It is incidental and varied. In this respect, I take occasional preaching to be something that is simultaneously timely and untimely. The sermons it offers might be said to take the form of a minor literature. It lives in a language that is not its own.[13] The occasional preacher speaks to a contemporary moment, an ordinary human encounter. But if she does so well, she helps to displace these moments from a logic of necessity. In so doing, she seeks to save us from the temptation to think that we might be able to save ourselves. In this way, her manner of speaking is inconvenient. Whether these sermons are successful in achieving these aims is for others to judge. But that, at any rate, is how I understand the collective task they are attempting to perform.

Finally, a word about the image that appears on the cover of the book. In the early years of the Christian church, the catacombs of Rome featured more depictions of the Jonah story than any other biblical or Christian image. The story of Jonah, and in particular the three days he spent in the belly of the giant fish, were thought to prefigure the three days when, as the Apostle's Creed puts it, Christ "descended to the dead." The Gospels of Matthew and Luke place this typological reading of the Jonah story in the mouth of Jesus himself. In Matthew's version, Jesus says, "for just as Jonah was three days and three nights in the belly of the sea monster, so for three days and three nights the Son of Man will be in the heart of the earth." (Matt 12:40) In time, the Christian tradition came to interpret Jonah's emergence from the belly of the fish as an anticipation of the resurrection of Christ.

In 18th Century Poland and the Czech Republic this christological reading of the Jonah story was incorporated into the form of some

---

[13] See Gilles Deleuze, *Kafka: Toward a Minor Literature*, trans. Dana Polan (Minneapolis: University of Minnesota Press, 1986), 19.

unusual looking pulpits that can still be found in many churches today. These pulpits are made in the form of the giant fish that swallowed Jonah after he was thrown from the ship and eventually spit him out onto the shore so that he could commence the prophetic work to which he had been called by God. We might refer to these as Jonah pulpits or fish pulpits. The pulpit that appears on the cover of this book is from the Church of Saints Peter and Paul in the small spa town of Duszniki-Zdrój in southwestern Poland, near the border with the Czech Republic. The donor of the pulpit was Johann Franz Heinel, who served as a parson of the church and is also thought to have conceived the basic design of the pulpit. The actual creation of the pulpit is attributed to the German sculptor Michael Kössler, who completed it around 1730 when the church was rebuilt. Kössler's version of the Jonah pulpit is more ornate and symbolically complex than most. Note, for example, the images of biblical writers and angelic messengers along with the messages delivered which adorn the fish and which might be described as a series of "holy barnacles."

In the most general sense, we might say that preaching from a Jonah pulpit is appropriate because just as Jonah is the figure who anticipated the key moments in the story of Christ, the sermon is likewise always pointing to Christ. But there is also something about the physical appearance of preaching from a Jonah pulpit that is equally important to consider. When delivering a sermon from such a pulpit, the preacher is positioned as if emerging from the mouth of the fish, much like the images of Jonah that adorn the walls of the Roman catacombs.[14] In this way, the very act of preaching replicates the position of Jonah at the moment he is being spit out onto the shore. The preacher is thus visually presented as one who is taking up the situation of Jonah as he finally comes to embrace his prophetic task of speaking on behalf of God. At the same time, Jonah's response to the call of God was hardly met with enthusiasm but rather sent him on a dramatic and arduous journey that was tinged with mix of fear, self-doubt, anger, and the inclination simply to flee. The visual effect of preaching from a Jonah pulpit might also be said to conjure up a fitting image of the difficulty of preaching I spoke of above. At the very least, I must confess that I often resonate with

---

[14] See for example this image of Jonah being spit out of the fish from the Catacombs of Sts. Marcellinus and Peter:
http://www.vatican.va/roman_curia/pontifical_commissions/archeo/images/giona_big.jpg

Jonah's initial impulse to flee when I am invited to preach. Because preaching is hard work. But the sermons collected in this book are evidence that, like Jonah, I eventually come around to embracing the invitation every now and then. I have never had the experience of preaching from a pulpit such as this one and likely never will. But it strikes me as a fitting image of the tumultuous range of sensations I experience on those occasions when I have accepted the invitation to preach.

Chapter 1

Beware, Keep Alert: On Advent and Idolatry[1]

Originally preached at Chapel Hill Mennonite Fellowship, Chapel Hill, NC
Nov. 30, 2008, First Sunday of Advent
Scripture Texts: Psalm 80:1-7, 17-19; Isaiah 64: 1-9; 1 Corinthians 1:3-9; Mark 13: 24-37

The first Sunday of Advent marks the beginning of the Christian year. So it would have been appropriate if we had greeted each other today with the recognition that a new year has begun. Among other things, doing so would remind us that Christian time is different than other ways of marking time. The fact that we do not give each other new year's greetings on the first Sunday of Advent can be taken to serve as a reminder that we generally live our lives according to a movement of time that is at odds with the time of the church. I suspect the everyday texture of our lives is determined as much by temporal markers such as the recent festival of consumerism that has come to be known as "Black Friday" as it is by Advent. It is no wonder we often find ourselves in a state of bewildering confusion. I make no promise to be able to undo that confusion. If anything, the collection of lectionary we have been given for this Sunday might add to our confusion by challenging some of the customary ways we have come to understand the season of Advent.

Let me begin by summarizing the general contours of what I want to say in a way that might seem somewhat counter-intuitive. The first and most basic point is that Advent is the most Jewish of Christian seasons. As Rowan Williams puts it, "in Advent. . .we all become. . .Jews

---

[1] An earlier version of this sermon was previously published as Chris K. Huebner, "Advent and Idolatry: A Sermon," *Vision: A Journal for Church and Theology* 12:1 (Spring 2011): 77-82. It is reprinted here with permission of the publisher. All rights reserved.

once more."[2] Yet we have become accustomed to approaching Advent in a way that strips it of its Jewish character. In so doing, we end up inhabiting a version of Christianity that is somehow fundamentally at odds with itself. That is to say, we end up with church that is insufficiently Christian precisely because it is not properly Jewish. And if such a church can be said to be at odds with itself, that is, paradoxically, because its identity has become far too clear, too pure, too smooth, too neat and tidy. In other words, it is at odds with itself precisely because it is not sufficiently at odds with itself.

A church that has lost a sense of the Jewish character of Advent loses the ability to wrestle with a particular set of tensions and ambiguities that are, I think, essential to its being the church. When Christianity eventually came to define itself over against Judaism, more than anything else it lost a robust sense of the messianic. Christianity's identification of Jesus as messiah has all too often had the effect of initiating an erasure of the very concept of the messiah. By "messianic," I mean to point to a sense of radical interruption—an inversion of the so-called "laws" of history, a revolutionary change that undoes and transforms the ways we have become accustomed to thinking and acting. It is this sense of interruption and revolutionary change that gives rise to the tensions and ambiguities I spoke of earlier. I will say more about this in a moment. For now, I want to suggest that all of this has to do with how we conceive of the relationship between Advent and Christmas. Let me try to explain.

We think of advent as a season of waiting. We speak of it by invoking notions of preparation and expectation, of anticipation and longing. This is entirely appropriate. Advent names an expectation of an event that is to come. It is a preparation for an arrival for which we are still waiting. So far, this is pretty straightforward. But things start to get difficult when we ask the necessary follow-up questions. What are we waiting for? And why do we wait? How are we to prepare for this event that is to come? What does our longing and expectation look like? What sort of posture does this waiting require?

The starting point from which we must attempt to answer these questions is, of course, the recognition that Advent is a time of preparation and waiting for Jesus, the messiah. But I am struck by how easy it is to think about this season in ways that minimize, even cancel

---

[2] Williams, *A Ray of Darkness*, 5.

out, a sense of the messianic character that is necessary if Jesus is to be what Christians traditionally confess him to be. We cancel out the logic of the messianic when we think of preparation and expectation in terms of a coming event that is somehow known in advance of its actual arrival. We cancel out the logic of the messianic when we think of the messiah as someone we will surely recognize. And we cancel out the logic of the messianic when we think of Advent as preparing for something for which *we* are still striving, a longing for something that *we* are responsible for bringing about.

But this approach is exactly what today's Old Testament texts warn us about. Notice that they both acknowledge the anger of God. They plead with God not to be angry, even though God has every right to be angry. The psalmist asks, "O Lord God of hosts, how long will you be angry with your people's prayers?" (Ps. 80:4) Isaiah appeals to God by pleading, "Do not be exceedingly angry, O Lord, and do not remember iniquity forever." (Isa. 64:9) Another way to put this is to note that these two texts perform a confession. They are acknowledgements that we have sinned. They turn upon a recognition of Israel's transgression and need for restoration.

Why is God angry? Why are the people of Israel in need of restoration? They are in need of restoration because they have taken their future into their own hands. They have tried to reach God on their own terms. They have become impatient. They have forgotten that their very existence rests upon their being chosen, called out from the nations. They have forgotten that God comes to God's people, not the other way around. They have, in short, failed to let God be God. Isaiah in particular is very clear about this. He emphasizes the fact that God arrives in ways we do not expect: "When you did awesome deeds that we did not expect, you came down, the mountains quaked at your presence. From ages past, no one has heard, no ear has perceived, no eye has seen any God besides you, who works for those who wait for him." (Isa. 64:34)

Notice the points of emphasis here: God's deeds are unexpected. God comes down. God works for those who wait. We cannot see or hear any God but God. Or rather, when we claim to see or hear God, we can be reasonably confident that it is not God whom we have seen or heard. This is why we are called to wait for God to come to us. If we rush to meet God, we invariably find something other than God. Paul's letter to the Corinthians echoes a similar theme: "God is faithful. *By him* you were called into the fellowship of the Son, Jesus Christ our Lord."

(1 Cor. 1:9, my italics) And the reading from the Gospel of Mark also reflects this conviction: "But about the day or hour, no one knows, neither the angels in heaven, nor the Son, but only the Father. Beware, keep alert; for you do not know when the time will come." (Mark 13:32-33)

How are we to make sense of these passages? I am struck by the sense of danger that seems to be underscored here. I suspect most of us do not think of Advent as a particularly dangerous time. But here we are told to beware, keep alert, and remain watchful. Danger is apparently lurking somewhere in all this. Might it be that the danger is us? I think we are being confronted with the fact of our apparently intractable human capacity for self-deception. In this respect, the danger might be said to remind us that our sense of ourselves and our place in relation to God and the world is not nearly as secure as we like to think it is.

As we enter into the time of expectation that is Advent, then, we are first of all being reminded of our sinfulness. We yearn for a messiah whom we will recognize. Or rather, we yearn for a messiah in whom we will recognize ourselves. We want a messiah who reflects what we would identify as best about ourselves. We long for a messiah who seems familiar, a friend we feel like we already know. But the scripture passages we have been given today seem to cut in exactly the opposite direction. They suggest that what we get is not a friend but a stranger. This is why Advent is dangerous: because it all too easily turns into a form of longing for and anticipation of the Jesus we think we've got figured out. It is exactly for this reason, I want to suggest, that we are called to beware, keep alert, and remain watchful.

We tend to think of Advent as a time when we gradually come closer to God, a God who comes to us in the human form we call Jesus. But Advent begins by confronting us with the anger of God. If these passages underscore anything, it might be said that they place the accent on God's distance or difference from us. The emphasis is not on a God with whom we are becoming increasingly familiar, but on a God who remains exceedingly strange. So it is in a spirit of confession that we come to this season. Advent is a time of preparation that calls us to confess our tendency to forget God, to turn God into something familiar.

Advent is the most Jewish of Christian seasons. It is Jewish in the sense that Judaism is framed by the question of idolatry. Advent is Jewish in the sense that it brings us face to face with our seemingly insatiable desire to erect idols. It is Jewish because it reminds us that our expectations will not be straightforwardly satisfied, that we will not get the messiah we think we are waiting for. It is Jewish because it emphasizes that God remains beyond our grasp, beyond our knowledge. It is Jewish because it reflects a longing that in some sense remains frustrated and endlessly deferred.

We often think of Advent as a sort of bridge we must traverse in order to arrive, once again, at that site of holiness called Christmas. We see Advent as a time when we move ever nearer to the presence of God. But this view gets it exactly the wrong way around. It turns the logic of the messianic inside-out. The lectionary readings we have heard today suggest that God is not something we reach, even when we do our best to get things right, even when we strive to be our holiest. Rather, the idea of the messianic is that God comes to us and in so doing radically transforms our entire way of being and thinking. Here Advent names a divine movement that interrupts and reorients us. If it names an expectation, it is of an event that will be explosive and disruptive—and thus profoundly unexpected.

How do we go about preparing for an Advent like this? I confess I do not have a ready answer. Indeed, I think the point of Christianity is that none of us does. But at the very least, an Advent like this seems to require a change in how we think about preparation. We often think of preparation as a gradual filling up, a process of addition or accumulation. In this sense, it could be described as a progressive unfolding that moves ever forward. Think, for example, of how we prepare for an exam by filling up our minds with the knowledge that we might reasonably be expected to deliver. But here we are presented with a rather different image of preparation. It is not so much a filling up as a kind of emptying. It is a matter not of addition but subtraction. It is a negative—perhaps even nihilistic—moment more than it is a positive or progressive one. That is because the messiah comes as much to defy our expectations as to satisfy them.

This is why Advent is so important. It serves to remind us that we have made Jesus all too familiar, perhaps even idolatrous. It reorients us to his profound strangeness. To quote Rowan Williams once again, it is "a way of learning again that God is God: that between even our deepest and holiest longing and the reality of God is a gap which only grace can cross."[3]

Another way to put all of this is to suggest that Advent ceases to be Advent when it becomes overdetermined by Christmas. Advent comes to be overdetermined by Christmas when we think that its point is to focus our gaze squarely on the event of Jesus' arrival. This is tempting because so much of our lives are governed by the metaphors of progress and accumulation I spoke of earlier. But what if Advent invites us to let our gaze be turned the other way around? Perhaps this also means that Christmas can only be Christmas if we can somehow unlearn what we think we already know about it. Might it be that this is why Advent precedes Christmas? The peculiarly Jewish character of Advent that we are wont to forget reminds us that we must unlearn the Jesus we think we know so that Jesus can come to us as messiah. Please note that this is not to suggest that we must become Jewish so that we can once again leave it behind as we embrace the Christianity of Christmas. Rather, it is to suggest that Christianity becomes unintelligible when it loses its profoundly Jewish character.

We tend to forget that the season of Advent has as much to do with the second coming of Jesus as it does with his "original" birth in Bethlehem. In doing so, we fail to grasp the sense in which it gives expression to the theological virtue of hope. And this forgetfulness is yet another symptom of how Christianity has abandoned the Jewish character of Advent. It assumes a kind of finality that distorts the structure of hope. Without the Jewishness of Advent, we are left with a most unchristian conception of Christmas. So let us work to reimagine Advent as a kind of confessing self-emptying, a hollowing out of our idolatrous temptations so that we can become ready to receive the gift that Christmas has to give—the unexpected gift of a messiah who comes to save us from the temptation that we must somehow save ourselves.

---

[3] Williams, *A Ray of Darkness*, 6.

Chapter 2

Strange Epiphanies

Originally offered as a chapel reflection at CMU
Jan. 6, 2005, Epiphany

Just when we've had about all the feasting we can handle during our celebration of Christmas, the Christian calendar goes and hits us up with another feast to celebrate. It's almost as if we are being taunted with the inevitable failure of those recently made—or perhaps re-made—New Year's resolutions, driven as they are by overly optimistic dreams of self-betterment or at least reduced waistlines. Apparently the church does not so much care about our lust for improved self-images, and so we get another feast thrown at us—the feast of the Epiphany. But of course, the feasts of the Christian calendar are not to be confused with those bloat-inducing gorge-fests that are typical of Mennonite family gatherings. Rather they are reminders of who we are, part of the ongoing work of forming and reforming the body of Christ. In this regard, it is interesting to consider why we should need another such reminder this soon after so crucial an event in the Christian year as Christmas. Might it be that the relation of Epiphany to Christmas is at least in part significant for the way it helps to correct for a tendency somehow to get the meaning of Christmas just a little bit skewed? At the very least we ought to appreciate that Epiphany is a necessary extension of the story of Christ's birth without which we somehow miss the full significance of Christmas. How is it that Epiphany reorients us to the strangeness of Christmas? Or better, how is it that Epiphany transforms the Christmas we've just finished celebrating, with all its comfortable sentimentality, into something far more profound and more profoundly unsettling.

We all know the story. Perhaps we know it all too well. So let us run the risk of repetition and be reminded once again. Christmas celebrates the incarnation of God in human form, the word become flesh. It takes place in Bethlehem amongst the shepherds, the people of David. It names, among other things, the radical particularity of God. Storied by

Christmas, we come to learn that the God of Christian worship is not a diffuse vapor that floats about defying the possibility of location, but a fleshy, embodied particular God, a God we may speak of as being present to us here, now. Christmas is the fulfillment of the messianic prophecies of the people of Israel. In that respect, it might be said to mark a kind of closure. It names the fulfillment of a series of very specific hopes, the culmination of a long-delayed set of expectations. Christmas is a celebration of the manifestation of God's presence among the people of God, the Jews.

And yet the story doesn't end there. We come, as we are reminded today, to the event known as the Epiphany.

The story of Epiphany stands in stark contrast to this way of capturing the meaning of Christmas. Indeed, I think it captures the sense in which the meaning of Christmas is not given to the possibility of being captured. Or at least it suggests that the meaning of Christmas cannot be captured in any straightforwardly final sort of way. In its most general sense, Epiphany celebrates the manifestation of God to the wise pagan visitors from the East. It is the story of another appearance of God, in this case not to the Jews but to the Gentiles. So if Christmas can be said to reflect a sense of closure, we might say that Epiphany marks a new and unpredictable sort of opening. If Christmas names the decisive moment of God's self-revelation, the fulfillment of messianic expectation, Epiphany might be seen as the explosion of this revelation. It is in many ways the suspension of the expectation whose fulfillment we have just witnessed—an explosion and a suspension that are so profoundly captured by Paul with his militant universalism, simultaneously particular and anti-particular, of neither Jew nor Greek, of love beyond the settlements of law. Epiphany is, in other words, a necessary reminder that the presence of God is not a presence that can somehow be contained by us. It draws attention to our inclination to find false comfort in a God who becomes present to us, a God of embodied particularity. Epiphany thus marks a disconcerting twist to many common ways of understanding the Christmas story. If Jesus's birth is the story of a gift that we have been given, Epiphany is a sobering reminder of our temptation to take that gift and turn it into a given over which we are somehow in control. It confronts us with our temptation to see the gift of Christ as a kind of held territory we are called upon to protect and secure. So Epiphany names a moment at which the gift of Christ, the truth of Christ, is snatched out of our control. Or rather, it is a reminder of what is at stake in coming to grips with its very character as gift. For gifts, in order to be gifts, must be unpredictable and unnecessary. They must be surprising and in some sense wild. They are not elicited in any direct way, not effected by the cause of some prior ordering.

We might describe Epiphany as a story in which the God who comes to satisfy particular messianic longings of the people of Israel also and unexpectedly appears to those whose longings looked very different. The Magi were, after all, chasing a star. They were scientists on a journey for order and predictability and they ended up being confronted with the anarchy of the manger and the cross. In other words, God does not merely come to us because of our longings that need to be fulfilled. God also comes in spite of our longings and in so doing works to unsettle them. Put differently, the point here is that it is not *our* hopes that God fulfils. Rather, we are speaking of the very transformation of hope so that we might be saved from the tyranny of those hopes that are grounded in what we like most about ourselves. As if to recognize that Christmas runs the risk of putting us to sleep with its sense of closure and fulfillment, Epiphany serves to awaken us to the radicalism of messianic expectation. Or rather, it reminds us of the sense in which this expectation is genuine only to the extent that it somehow continues. In other words, it reminds us that messianic expectation is the sort of expectation that goes wrong when we attempt to pin it down too finally. We are here being confronted with a notion of time that cannot be plotted out in a step-by-step plan, and whose unfolding we cannot strategically direct with linear, instrumental calculations of cause and effect. We might say that Christmas pushes us in the direction of the so-called cataphatic tradition in Christian theology that emphasizes presence and the possibility of positive speech about God. Epiphany, then, counters with a nod toward the apophatic tradition of negative theology, with its stress on the absence and mystery of God, its appreciation of the sense that God can only be spoken of in terms of what God is not.

I suspect at this point that it might be good to remind ourselves that all of this is cause for celebration. It calls for a feast day. It is part of the good news. Or at least that is what the liturgical structure of the church calendar seems to be telling us. It might help, here, to point to a certain sense of duality which is built into the very notion of celebration, a duality that I suspect is too often missed when we focus on celebrations

21

like Christmas. At one level—perhaps the more straightforward level—celebration functions as a sort of commemoration, an act of memory. It is the repetition of something we already know and appreciate. But there is another level of celebration that pushes us beyond mere memory, and highlights its dangerous potential for sedimentation and ossification. Here celebration can be described as ecstatic. It takes us into new and uncharted territory. Sometimes the point of celebration is not to find ourselves, not to remember who we are, but rather to lose ourselves, and in this very loss taught to find ourselves once again, to remember who we are in new and more profound ways. If we are tempted to see Christmas as a celebration in the memorial sense of the term, I think it is important to see Epiphany as a celebration of the ecstatic variety. Or perhaps a better way to put it would be to say that Epiphany is the kind of celebration that properly trains us to see Christmas as a celebration both of memory and ecstasy.

I offer all this as a series of gestures that I hope might go some way toward constituting a theological commentary on our chapel theme for the year. For it is this theme that I have been asked to speak about today. "When the spirit of truth comes. . . ." I must confess that when I first heard about it, I wasn't exactly thrilled about this particular choice for a theme. In short, I worried that it was just a little bit too comforting. It seemed to give the impression that the kind of truth we're talking about here at CMU is somehow going to be easy, as if we don't have to work at it, as if it does not name a struggle. But in the course of preparing these reflections, I have come to see it in a somewhat different light. And so I close with a few remarks about my newfound appreciation for our theme, an appreciation sparked by this celebration of the feast of the Epiphany.

"When the spirit of truth comes. . . ." Note first, that it says when, not if. We are told that the truth is coming. There is nothing we can do to screw it up completely. This is good news. But of course there is also a flipside. Just as there's nothing we can do to screw it up, it is also the case that there is nothing we can do to guarantee its arrival either. This too is good news. Second, notice also the other sense of the word "when," as in still to come. Here we are being reminded that the truth is not something of which we are fully in possession. It is not something we can be said to grasp. We must continue to expect it. And we are being called here to learn how to live into that sense of expectation. Third, we are reminded that the truth that is to come is the work of the Spirit. It is the work of the one who arrives to unsettle and disturb as much as to comfort and console. Or rather, it is the work of one who comforts and consoles precisely by disturbing the self-directed gazes we habitually cast upon both ourselves and others. Finally, perhaps the overall key to the passage we have adopted as this year's chapel theme is captured by the ellipsis that wrests it, some might say violently, from its original home in the gospel of John. It hangs here in a kind of ongoing suspense, gracefully haunting us as it forces us to confront our desire for closure. Let us imagine that it is suspended somewhere between Christmas and Epiphany. For this, let us celebrate.

Chapter 3

And the Greatest of These is Love

Originally preached at Fort Garry Mennonite Fellowship, Winnipeg, MB
February 1, 2004, Fourth Sunday of Epiphany
Scripture texts: Jeremiah 1: 4-10; Psalm 71: 1-6; 1 Corinthians 13: 1-13; Luke 4: 21-30

    "And the Greatest of these is love." (1 Cor. 13:13) I suspect many of us hear these words of Paul and find our thoughts naturally drifting toward the familiar scene of a naively optimistic and blissfully happy wedding day. We think of young couples with their entire lives lying promisingly head of them who are drawn to this text as a symbolic cornerstone on which to base their future lives together. The flowers are lush and radiant. The music is moving and flawlessly performed. Everybody looks stunningly beautiful. And all of these things conspire to create a mood which is pregnant with heady anticipation. Or at least that is where I find myself being taken whenever I hear Paul's remarks about love. I would be surprised if I were the only one here who has heard a wedding sermon or two based on these words from Paul's letter to the church in Corinth. There may even be couples among us this morning whose marriages were performed against the background of a reading of this passage. If so, I should perhaps offer a word of apology in advance, just in case any of the things I am about to say is taken in the wrong way. Because it ends up being chosen by so many adoring young couples, this has arguably become one of the most well-known passages in the entire Bible. And yet precisely because we have become accustomed to hearing these words in the context of a wedding ceremony, I suspect it is equally one of the most systematically distorted, misunderstood, and perhaps even self-deceptive of biblical texts.

    We naturally tend to read this passage in a manner that seeks to take us to a place of good feelings. The love spoken of here is a romanticized love whose function it is to be comforting and self-confirming. In the process, love is seen primarily as an emotion, one which we identify as a necessary condition of our happiness. We all yearn for someone to love and to love us back, someone to complete us and make our lives whole. In this sense, love becomes a refuge, a goal to be longed after, and a source of strength. And there is, of course, a sense in which all of this is entirely appropriate.

But we need to be careful at precisely this point. So let us take another look. It is instructive, I take it, that the lectionary selection for today, the fourth Sunday after Epiphany, places this text in the company of a series of others which are anything but comforting. First, we hear the prophet Jeremiah telling us that the call of the Lord is to rule "over nations and kingdoms, to pluck up and pull down, to destroy and overthrow, and [only then] to build and plant." (Jeremiah 1:10) We habitually find ourselves drawn to Paul's emphasis on love because we see love as an unreservedly positive thing. It builds us up, provides us with some heart-warming comfort, and in doing so makes us strong. And yet here we are being confronted with a profoundly negative message of destruction and judgement. Jeremiah's words are not a celebration of strength, but rather a warning that the strong and comforting realities in which we place our trust—the nations and the kingdoms, as he refers to them—will be torn down and overthrown. By placing Paul alongside Jeremiah, are we perhaps being led to a similar warning about how we conceive of love? The passage from Luke would seem to confirm such a suspicion. It provides us with an account of how Jesus' message of love was such that "when they heard this, all in the synagogue were filled with rage." (Luke 4: 28) Indeed, we are told that he inspired such furious indignation that they "drove him out of town, and led him to the brow of the hill on which their town was built, so that they might hurl him off the cliff." (Luke 4: 29) Again, there seems to be something counter-intuitive going on here. We see love as a happy emotion, one which is supposed to overcome hatred and strife. And yet when Jesus spoke of love, it was said to provoke the kind of extreme anger and rage that would lead an audience to kill the one who preached it. Whatever else is going on in Jeremiah and Luke, it seems fair to conclude that they are hardly happy texts. So what is being suggested by placing Paul's words on love in the context of these other passages? They certainly cast our understanding of love in a significantly different light. If Paul tells us that love is patient and kind, it seems that Jeremiah and Luke are enlisted to suggest that this is a wild patience and a threatening sort of kindness. As if responding to the temptation to read Paul in romantic and escapist terms, Jeremiah and Luke bring us face to face with some much needed harsh reality.

So what is going on here? In one sense, I think it might be seen as an attempt to help us identify and resist the tendency to idolize love. Encouraged by the all-too-familiar refrains of mainstream popular culture—whether Christian or otherwise—we have become accustomed to placing our hope in sentimentalized conceptions of love. "All you need is love," we sing along with the Beatles. Or, with Huey Lewis in his theme song for the hit movie *Back to the Future*, we proclaim that it's the "power of love" that "makes the world go 'round'." But before long, we find that we have, like Robert Palmer, simply become addicted to love. I apologize to those whose musical knowledge is more recent than mine. But I'm sure you can supply similar examples of your own. In doing so, we simultaneously overstate the value of love and reduce it to a rather shallow, self-affirming emotion. Like all addictions, I suspect that in lusting after love in this way we end up doing little more than deceiving ourselves in the name of short-term pleasure. But Paul seems to present love as a hedge against self-deception. For he tells us that "love rejoices in the truth." (1 Cor. 13:6) To get closer to the truth, however, we need to pay attention to that counter-tradition which presents us with an alternative to mainstream popular music, namely genuine country music. Not the saccharine over-produced garbage that so often comes out of Nashville these days, but the kind of music associated with Hank Williams and Johnny Cash. Or perhaps with Gram Parsons and Emmylou Harris, who redirect our attention to the sense in which "love hurts." Or Lucinda Williams, whose raw and jarring voice achingly reminds us that we do not live in a "world without tears." Genuine love paradoxically needs tears. As Lucinda Williams puts it, "if we lived in a world without tears. . .how would misery know which back door to walk through, . . .how would scars find skin to etch themselves onto, . . .and how would trouble know which mind to live inside of?" How, in other words, might we live lives that could properly be called human? Where popular music can be said to alienate us from our very humanity, country music brings us back in touch with our status as creatures.

Please note that this is not to suggest that we ought to do away with love altogether. Nor is it a perverse attempt to glorify suffering. Rather, I am suggesting that good country music is best understood as a counter-cultural attempt to resist what we might call the misanthropic hegemony of love. It is a stark reminder of how badly things can go wrong if we make an idol out of love. And this is what Paul is ultimately telling us too, even if we seem destined to distort his words in the name of our idolatry of love. In other words, we misunderstand Paul if we read him as suggesting that love alone is the key to salvation. Love will not save us, God will. Which is but another way of saying that being a Christian means loving as God loves, not turning to love as a way of saving ourselves.

In order to make some sense of what it might mean to speak of loving as God loves, we need to reflect on the profound ambiguity and fragility of love. On the one hand, to remember the tensions that love elicits ought to be relatively straightforward to any of us who have dared to risk loving another. For love hardly names an enterprise which is assured of success. And yet we often become experts at blinding ourselves to the way in which our love often fails us. Love is surely one of the most complex aspects of human existence. On the one hand, love seems to be what we all long for, perhaps more than even money, fame, or the assurance of security. And yet at the same time, love seems to beckon us, perhaps even taunt us, into venturing into dangerous and radically unpredictable territory. Love pulls us like a magnet toward the truth. And so we open our hearts and share our deepest confessions with one another. And yet in doing so, too many of us find that we are confronted with the difficult task of having to deal with intense feelings of hurt and betrayal. We find ourselves fumbling around with the complex grammar of love as we attempt to give expression to our most profound triumphs. And yet it is that same grammar of love to which we are drawn in an attempt to reveal the deep wounds that cut to the very core of human life.

Perhaps more than anything else, it is love that makes us aware of the radical vulnerability which penetrates and pierces our relationships with one another. Think of those three seemingly innocent words, "I love you." From infancy, we are trained to let these words slip so easily from our lips, just as we habitually seek to elicit them from the mouths of others. And yet these very same words can function as some of the most coercive and violent words in the English language. Too often, it seems, our proclamations of love for one another do little more than serve as a mask by which we conceal our attempts to manipulate one another. We tell our loved ones that we love them, and find that in doing so we are tangled up in intricate webs of power in which we play games that seek to use the other for our own good. Love is undeniably the most powerful of human longings. And because of this we find that it is all-too-easily open to abuse. On first blush, it seems so straightforward and simple. But when we are more honest with ourselves we find that love is a profoundly ambiguous and fragile form of human expression. It is as easily given to wounding as it is to providing a sense of healing.

At the risk of sounding too depressing, I want to suggest that there is a sense in which this woundedness of love is precisely the point of the Christian tradition. I do not mean to claim that we are destined to be crushed and broken under the cruel weight of love. Rather, as Rowan Williams so wonderfully puts it, to focus on love in this way is to help us appreciate that "at the very centre of ourselves will be something fragile."[1] We seem naturally inclined to think of the self as having a centre that is a site of power and strength, a smaller version of the nations and kingdoms that Jeremiah spoke of. Notice how this describes the way in which the category of "identity" is often invoked. We like to speak of our lives as if they are somehow possessions over which we are fully in control. We like to see ourselves as self-sufficient entities, as the sole originators of the activities and desires which we think define us. But we do well to remind ourselves that the Christian language of the self gains its intelligibility through what we might call the grammar of creaturehood. To see oneself as a creature is to come to appreciate that we are not finally in control of our lives. To speak of a creature, in other words, is to imply a creator. Which is but another way of saying that our very existence in the first place is due to an exceedingly generous and unsolicited gift of another. So the grammar of creaturehood helps us to appreciate that the self is not finally a possession to be protected or a territory to be secured. It is, rather, a gift to be given to others which is equally constituted by its ability to receive gifts from others in turn. Our lives are not finally to be understood in terms of categories of self-sufficiency, but by vulnerable inter-dependence. The most important thing about our lives is not that we are strong and powerful but that we are frail and feeble. These are the sorts of descriptions that help to flesh out what Paul is getting at in drawing our attention to the greatness of love.

It is at this point that we need to fix our attention more firmly than we have so far on the example of Jesus. For God's becoming human in

---

[1] Williams, *A Ray of Darkness*, 35.

Jesus is perhaps more than anything else a new way of thinking about power from the perspective of vulnerability. The story of Jesus is the story of one who experienced "a sense of the *precariousness* of goodness, love, and fidelity so profound and strong that no failure or error could provoke his condemnation, except the error of those legalists who could not understand that very precariousness."[2] At the same time, we find in Jesus a paradigm for how we are to relate to one another. Most importantly, we ought to recognize that Jesus responds to others not by violently exercising power over them, but by humbling himself. Jesus does not resort to power by force, but redefines power as a form of charity and love. It is not accidental, I take it, that we are being asked to reflect on these themes at this point in the church's calendar. We are in the time of Epiphany, the extended period of God's self-appearing. We are living in the time between Christmas and Easter, between incarnation and resurrection. Too often, I suspect, we think of Christmas and Easter in ways that seem to imply cancelling out the reality of crucifixion. But it is the cross which lies hauntingly between Christmas and Easter. It is the *crucified* lord which is the resurrected lord. And so we misunderstand the nature of Christian love if we overstate it in such a way that reinforces our tendency to seek strength and security in the same old ways that Jeremiah warned us against.

We do well to remember that Paul was not speaking of love in a context that would have us think first of couples and weddings. Rather, Paul draws our attention to love in the midst of a reflection on the kind of life together we have come to describe as church. Paul is reminding the people of the church in Corinth what kind of people they have been called to be. He is giving them counsel on how they ought to live amongst one another in order to claim their allegiance to Christ. In doing so, Paul seems to be suggesting that the church is a place where we learn to be appropriately vulnerable to one another. Too often, however, we think of the church as a place of refuge in which we define ourselves in terms of familiarity and sameness over against the threats of some conception of the external world. We prefer to secure identity in the way that Paul's audience was said to secure their identities as Jews over against those who laid claim to being Greek. But Paul speaks of the church as a place in which there is no Jew, nor Greek. In doing so, Paul is pointing to a love which works not because it allows us to secure

---

[2] Ibid., 11.

identity over against difference. Rather, that conception of Christian identity which is founded on love is meaningful precisely because it is constituted by difference. This is hardly a sentimental, comfortable, and self-confirming love. On the contrary, it is a radical, life-transforming and counter-cultural form of love. It is a love which is tested by nothing less than the possibility of extending hospitality to the stranger, of being open to the least of these, and of loving even the enemy.

So what we are confronted with here is a reflection on the profound strangeness of God's love. Too often, our reflections on love are driven by a tendency to have things settled. We are motivated to seek out comforts and so to have things made easily manageable. But the love which Paul calls the greatest is not this sort of love. On the contrary, it is a decidedly contrarian and unsettling form of love. It seeks not to encourage a cozy sense of comfort, but to rescue us from the temptation to pursue those loves which reinforce what we like most about ourselves. Paul's love is not first of all a good-feeling emotion, but a political way of understanding how to inhabit forms of life together with others. And even though we need to get here by debunking many of the standard myths of love, this is not finally a message of despair but of hope. To acknowledge the vulnerable fragility of our lives is one of the more significant conditions of the biblical view of liberation. We seek to tame and domesticate love, or at least to turn to love in an attempt to find a place of secure refuge from the rest of our confusing lives. In other words, we set limits to love and turn to love in an attempt to set out the manageable limits of our lives. But to speak of love as Paul did, to learn to love as Jesus did, is to expose the error of our attempts to set easily enforceable limits on love. It is to save us from the error of thinking that we can somehow steer our way safely through the choppy waters of love. "And the greatest of these is love." Let us live among one another in such a way that these words might ring true.

Chapter 4

The Problem of the Familiar Jesus
and the Task of Understanding

Originally offered as a chapel reflection at CMU
February 28, 2012

The Gospel of Matthew is often referred to a wisdom book. It locates the good news of the gospel in the context of the biblical wisdom tradition—a tradition which assumes that there is a discernible order to the created world that can be said somehow to reflect the mind of God. To be in communion with God is to be in a position to understand the complex workings of the world. This concern with wisdom is arguably at the heart of Chapter 13, from which our chapel theme for the year has been drawn. Here we see Jesus presented as a teacher, providing instruction both to large crowds and to his close followers about what the kingdom of heaven is like. He is also presented as one who is concerned to make sure his audience understands the significance of his teachings. He worries that while his crowd appears to be listening attentively, they do not fully understand what he is talking about. Indeed, this is the reason he gives for turning to the parables of the kingdom in the first place. He seems to think that parables might be a medium better suited for those who, unlike the disciples, "do not know the secrets of the kingdom of heaven." And yet even the disciples find themselves needing to come to Jesus for further instruction. And when he is finished explaining the parables to them, he interrogates their capacity for understanding as well: "Have you understood all this?" he asks them. And, like a class of CMU students, whose deference is matched only by their capacity for succinct speech, they answer with a simple "Yes."

Given this concern with the themes of wisdom and understanding, it is hardly surprising that this chapter wound up being chosen for a series of reflections in the context of a university. The Jesus we meet here sounds very much like a professor relating to a classroom full of eager to learn university students. In other words, the Jesus we meet here is an entirely familiar Jesus—familiar at least to those of us immersed in the world of the university. Now here is a Jesus with whom we find ourselves able to relate. I know I can. Speaking to a crowd that appears to be listening and yet worrying that they do not entirely understand what they are hearing? Welcome to my world. Or my nightmare, whatever the case may be. But isn't that precisely the problem? Not my world or my nightmares, I mean, though these may well be problematic too. Rather, the problem is with a Jesus who is all too familiar.

The problem of the familiar Jesus. Now why would I call this a problem? Isn't this exactly what we want? Aren't we all looking for a Jesus we can relate to? Go to any Christian bookstore and you will see this reflected in the shelves full of Bibles that cater to every possible demographic. Or if you don't frequent those sorts of pious places, you can find the same thing reflected among more politically minded Christians with their neatly codified patterns of discipleship and their programmatic manuals for conflict resolution or development work. Both forms of Christianity, it seems to me, are driven by the need to find a Jesus that is maximally familiar. And yet at the same time, it might be said that this desire for a familiar Jesus is responsible for draining the life out of the contemporary church in North America, even in those places that might appear to be bursting at the seams—whether they be mega churches or occupy movements. Allow me to indulge in a brief digression in order to illustrate.

In writing these words, I couldn't help but think about a recent song by Craig Finn, who normally performs with the Hold Steady but who has just released a solo album. Finn is not only a great lyricist and performer. He is also one of the more astute commentators on contemporary North American Christianity. The song is called "New Friend Jesus." And I think it can be heard as an attempt to point to what I have called the problem of the familiar Jesus. Let me read the lyrics to the first verse: "Everybody's saying that the lights don't shine, but the light shines down on me. I got a new friend and my new friend's name is Jesus. I met him in the parking lot, he took me in his car. I got a new friend and my new friend's name is Jesus. We rode around all afternoon, he sold me his guitar. I got a new friend and my new friend's name is Jesus. Now people give me sideways looks when we set up on the Strand. It's hard to suck with Jesus in your band." You get the point. This is a Jesus who is almost uncomfortably too familiar, too close, maybe a bit like Judge Reinhold as the infamous "close talker" in that well-known *Seinfeld* episode. My new friend Jesus likes the same things (guitars and bands and driving around) and he makes it possible to survive a world full of haters. He understands me perfectly, just as I understand him. It is the haters who just don't understand. On the one hand, you can see the appeal. Who isn't looking for allies to help survive a world full of haters? But isn't there something a little bit hollow, or at least adolescent, about a Jesus who is familiar in this sort of way?

It is not just Craig Finn and cynical university professors who find the familiarity of Jesus and the sort of understanding reflected by him to present somewhat of a problem. This problem is also signaled in the Chapter from Matthew we are talking about. After the disciples assure Jesus that yes, they understand all that he was teaching them, Jesus leaves and returns to his hometown to spend some time teaching the people in the synagogue there. Matthew tells us that "they were astounded and said, 'where did this man get this wisdom and these deeds of power?' . . . And they took offense at him. But Jesus said to them, 'Prophets are not without honor except in their own country and in their own house.'" Here Matthew seems to be signaling that the sort of wisdom and understanding associated with Jesus is precisely not the sort of thing we would describe as immediately familiar. In fact, it is entirely unfamiliar and foreign, at least to those who were ostensibly most familiar with him. That is why he gets run out of his home synagogue. And it explains why he would be perpetually worried about the capacity of his audience to understand. Wisdom is not easy. It is strange and difficult. It is hostile to the familiar. It is foreign, reflecting a posture of the exile rather than the one who exists safely within the comforts of home.

Is this not what we are to hear when Jesus laments to his disciples that it is entirely possible to see things and yet not really to perceive, to listen and yet not really hear? To put it somewhat differently, it is possible to utter true words and yet to speak falsely. In fact, the art of modern politics is arguably based on precisely this sort of pseudo-skill. And finally, it is possible to gain all kinds of knowledge and yet not to understand. If there is a single thread that runs through Chapter 13, it is this distinction between mere knowledge and full understanding. And it is the possibility that these two should come unhinged that should serve to haunt a place like CMU.

When Matthew identifies Jesus as a figure of wisdom, he is drawing attention to the sense in which this sort of wisdom interrupts and radically transforms what normally counts as knowledge. Just as the politics of the exile interrupts and radically transforms an imagination in which politics is equated with the pursuit of sovereignty, so the exiled wisdom of Jesus challenges the assumption that knowledge might be spoken of as a form of mastery, possession, or control. The wisdom of Jesus does not speak of knowledge as a possession of some sort. Wisdom is not a form of knowledge we might be said to have or hold on to. Rather, it is an inherently dispossessive form of knowledge. It does not name a journey in which we yearn to secure a safe passage home. On the contrary, it actively seeks to include the stranger and in so doing complicates how we understand what we call home. It is genuine just to the extent that it is haunted by the unfamiliar. So when it comes to the question of understanding, it would seem that this is a form of understanding that is perpetually unsettled. As Rowan Williams notes, this sort of wisdom is not so much about taking a position on a particular subject matter in the hope that it might one day be vindicated as true. It is more a matter of learning how to be placed "in a certain kind of relationship to truth, such that we can be changed by it."[1] Williams suggests that in order to appreciate the wisdom with which Matthew identifies Jesus, we must not miss "the underlying darkness of Matthew's apparently ordered mental world."[2] I am suggesting that this sense of underlying darkness is exactly what gets obscured when we pursue what I am calling the familiar Jesus.

All of this should lead us to come back to the "yes" that the disciples provided in answer to Jesus's question, "Have you understood all this?" I think the question that needs to be asked here is what is the status of this "yes"? I don't know about you, but I am led to wonder whether this "yes" might not be like so many of the moustaches we see around campus these days—that is to say more ironic than serious. Do the disciples in fact understand Jesus? Or is Matthew here signaling that even the disciples fail to understand, just to the extent that they are so quick to tell him that they do. This strikes me as a more fitting segue to the scene of exile that immediately follows, where Jesus and his wisdom are run out of their hometown. To put it somewhat differently, what if Jesus's question "Have you understood all this?" is better read as functioning like a trick question, a question that fails just to the extent that you can find an easy answer for it. To read this chapter as a whole, it seems to me that we should approach the possibility of understanding

---

[1] Williams, *Christ on Trial*, 39.
[2] Ibid., 28.

the kingdom of heaven more along the lines of the way Augustine speaks about the possibility of understanding God: "if you have understood, then what you have understood is not God."[3]

What does any of this have to do with the parables of the kingdom of heaven? To this I want to suggest that it has both nothing and everything to do with these parables. Let me explain. To put this in context, I should say that I was assigned the task of picking one of these parables and reflecting on what it might mean to say the kingdom of heaven is like a mustard seed or like yeast or like a hidden treasure. But the more I thought about the task, the more I came to think that I could not successfully complete that task. Why is this? Because I wonder whether the wisdom reflected in this collection of parables is such that it is not contained in any one of them taken individually. Nor do I think it is best to understand the parables functioning like singular bits of wisdom that might be accumulated in order to flesh out something we might think of as an overall picture. What if the wisdom here is reflected precisely in the difference between the various parables? In other words, what if the point of offering so many parables of the kingdom is precisely to frustrate the desire to think we can fit them into a single whole? If we read the parables this way, then notice how the force of the message changes in such a way that any sense of likeness that can be said to exist among them is immediately qualified by the realization that there is a greater sense of unlikeness. In that case, the wisdom of Jesus might be understood as an attempt to expose the falsehood of approaching the kingdom of heaven as if it were something about which we must accumulate positive knowledge in some sort of straightforward way. In this respect, we might say that the kingdom of heaven is, like Jesus, essentially mysterious and constitutively unfamiliar.

In closing, I want to return to the question of haters I mentioned earlier. What if the polemical context of the good news is not so much about surviving the haters that our new friend Jesus helps us endure? What if the point is, rather, to help us appreciate that we are the haters? What if our love of Christ—our praising and exalting, our peace and justice—masks an underlying hatred of Christ, the stranger, just as our so-called knowledge conceals a lack of understanding? Start reckoning with these sorts of questions and I think we are well on our way to being schooled in the sort of wisdom Matthew saw in Jesus. We might even

---

[3] This is Elizabeth Johnson's way of glossing Augustine's formula for speaking about God. See Johnson, *She Who Is*, 170.

be on our way to that altogether strange and foreign land Jesus describes as the kingdom of heaven.

Chapter 5

What I Learned in Jerusalem: A Faith Story

Originally offered as a chapel reflection at CMU
March 7, 2014

I will always remember the feeling of wading through that knee-deep water. Occasionally, the water would get a little deeper and eventually it was necessary to let go of the instinct to try and remain completely dry. And since the rocky ground was uneven and more than a little slippery, we had to watch our steps pretty carefully in order to avoid taking an inadvertent and very cold bath. Sometimes the obstacles came from the other direction as the ceiling pushed down low enough that it forced us at least to consider the possibility that the critical distance between it and the water might suddenly vanish altogether. And then there was the darkness. It was so thick you could almost feel it pressing in on you, somehow making it a bit difficult to breathe. Of course, the little candles we'd been given all got blown out at a certain point. Darkness like that is just too tempting for 12 year olds not to try and see what they can get away with. The first time I walked through the dark, water-filled passageway it was simultaneously terrifying and exhilarating. Eventually, Hezekiah's Tunnel in the old City of David just outside of Jerusalem's Old City came to be one of my favourite places. There was something just plain crazy about it. Sloshing through a meandering tunnel that was hewn out of the rock some 2000 plus years ago to provide a source of water in light of an impending siege. Who does this? It became a must see destination on my own little tourist itineraries to which I would subject the many visitors that passed though Jerusalem for the two years that we lived there.

As far as wandering around in the dark goes, Hezekiah's Tunnel proved to be pretty safe. There was really only one way you could go, namely straight ahead. Things could get a bit sketchy if you met the wrong company coming from the other direction. But it's not like you could get altogether lost. Keep sloshing through the dark water and eventually you will see the light starting to shine at the other end of the tunnel. There were other places I liked to explore. Another one was called the King's Tomb. It consisted of a series of burial chambers hewn from the rock. The story I recall—I have no idea whether it is true or not—is that most of them were fake, designed to outsmart potential grave robbers. Among the many covered openings leading from the main chamber, most of them didn't go anywhere. But one of them led, through a maze of other passages, to the real tomb. Of course, even the real tomb was empty by the time we got there. It seems the plan to outsmart the robbers did not work. But that is in keeping with one of the most profound lessons you learn when living in Jerusalem. If there is one thing that Christians, Jews, and Muslims share with each other, not to mention Winnipeg Jets fans, it is that faithfulness is in no way straightforwardly related to success. Or rather, what we call success often comes about in spite of our best efforts, not because of them.

The thing I remember most fondly about living in Jerusalem is just the wandering around and exploring. I loved trying to get lost in the Old City, scampering around its numerous small markets and twisting alleys, its thick walls and dark corners, hoping to stumble upon some exciting new discovery as I tried to find my way back out to one of the gates. There were, of course, all manner of official holy sites to explore as well. But I seem to have had a preference for the more ordinary and minor places—call them secular spaces—that Jerusalem has to offer. I found myself drawn to exploring sites that were comparably more marginal or in some ways entirely absent from the stories you learn in places like Sunday School and mainstream tourist itineraries.

In a wonderful stroke of good fortune, some of this wandering was even officially sanctioned. There was a class at the school I attended called "Jerusalem Studies." It was far and away my favourite course at the Anglican School in Jerusalem. In part, I suspect, that is because it had no real point, no heady pedagogical agenda. There was no specifiable goal we had to reach in order to make it to the next grade. There were no learning objectives or outcomes, so to speak, beyond nurturing a spirit of adventure. That there were no assignments to hand in may have also played a large role in my appreciation of the course. But mostly I saw it as another opportunity to wander around Jerusalem and explore its many interesting sites. If I had any sort of career ambitions at the time, I was pretty sure I wanted to become an archaeologist. Or course, this may have also had something to do with the fact that *Raiders of the Lost Ark* was one of the more popular movies at the time. But mostly I enjoyed digging through everything this strange new world seemed to be offering me.

"Christianity: It's not a religion. It's an adventure." Moreover, it's "an adventure we didn't know we wanted to be on."[1] Or so my friend and former teacher Stanley Hauerwas is fond of saying. Among other things, Hauerwas is suggesting that Christianity is distorted if we think of it as a kind of inner phenomenon known as a religious experience. Christianity, he argues, is far richer, thicker, and way more confusing than that. More than anything, it's about a people—a people who do not fully understand what it is that constitutes them as a people such that they do not lay claim to a settled identity of some sort. To the extent that I have a faith story at all, I want to say that it's only because I find myself claimed by such a people. Being Christian is about being "part of a community that transforms our desires toward things we did not know we wanted."[2] But it is important to acknowledge the rather counter-intuitive conception of community that is in play here. In so far as there is a community here, it is a diffuse and episodic one—a community spread across place and time and includes people who did not know each other. It is a community, in other words, that seems to keep disappearing and coming back. To borrow an image from the political philosopher Sheldon Wolin, we might describe this sort of community as fugitive.[3] The church is a community that is always under threat by forces that would strive to manage it. Among those forces, the most significant and dangerous will to manage is that which comes from within the church herself. One significant implication of such a claim is that the story of Christianity has a way of showing up in places where we might not expect to find it. Among those places, of course, are those that would not normally be counted as "Christian" in any meaningful way. I would not have put it this way, of course, while I was splashing through Hezekiah's tunnel or imagining myself among the grave robbers in the King's Tomb. But if I can say I have learned anything about how to be Christian, I suspect I learned much of it in Jerusalem.

I moved with my family to Jerusalem in the summer of 1981. I was 12 years old. Ronald Reagan had recently been elected president of the

---

[1] Hauerwas, "Christianity: It's Not a Religion, It's an Adventure," 531.

[2] Ibid., 522.

[3] For a helpful reflection on the theological significance of Wolin's notion of fugitivity, see Dula, Cavell, Companionship, and Christian Theology, 95-113.

United States. And while I remember some adults speculating about how this probably meant an impending nuclear war with the Soviets was just around the corner, I never really sensed the significance of the threat. And in any case, things did not play out as those adults speculated they might. I suppose this should be considered good news. And yet when we arrived in Jerusalem, the presence of war, or at least the very real possibility of violence, was never all that far away. For example, our school did not have fire drills. We had air raid drills in which we would all file into an old underground cistern or time ourselves to see how quickly we could dive beneath our desks to take cover. Driving in and around Jerusalem meant navigating armed checkpoints and sometimes having our car searched by soldiers who seemed to delight in the terror they could elicit simply by flashing their massive guns in our faces.

And sometimes those soldiers weren't just nameless and abstract symbols of war. I remember one time when I was wandering around the old city when I came upon my guitar teacher in military fatigues carrying an Uzi while guarding the entrance to some building. I knew it theoretically, but somehow this drove home the point that being a soldier was just something that some people had to do in the course of their daily life in Jerusalem. I will never forget the strangeness of life during the Israeli incursion into Lebanon and the massacre at Sabra and Shatila refugee camps in the fall of 1982. I remember how at school there was a visceral, disorienting sense of confusion—a confusion located in the gut rather than the mind—that somehow life went on as normal even as we knew it was not at all close to being normal. Some of my friends had parents who were stationed in Lebanon as peacekeepers with the United Nations and they would share reports that stood in stark contrast to the official stories that were being circulated by the mainstream media at the time. More than anything else, this drove home the point that war is not just something you read about in history books or hear about on the news. It is very real and not always very far from home. But at the same time, we were still thirteen. I don't know if Jerusalem was the only place in the world where a warm-up run during gym class would spontaneously turn into that scene from the movie *Stripes* with a bunch of kids singing Do Wah Diddy Diddy as if they were marching alongside Bill Murray and John Candy. But that's the sort of thing that went down at the school I attended. Even as we were trying to make sense of the fact that we were living in a world of war, our lives were still punctuated by a very real sense of adolescent humour. If nothing else, living in strange times like these means you never get bored.

Among the most important lessons I learned in Jerusalem was that religious identities constitute differences that are very real, but equally difficult to pin down. Being Christian or Jewish is not just a matter of subscribing to a different collection of beliefs that somehow reside in the mind. It makes a difference for how you go about your daily life in the world. Indeed, it makes a difference for how the world is constituted in the first place. There is one incident in particular that drove this point home for me. I was walking back home by myself from the Mennonite Central Committee offices up on the hill to our home in the valley. In Jerusalem, the ground is never flat and the roads are even less straight. And besides, to stick to the roads meant for a very long walk. So I would often take a shortcut through a set of stairways that led through a section of poorer Palestinian homes that dotted the side of the hill. One day I came around the corner and evidently startled a Palestinian boy who was about the same age as I was. Given my appearance, he naturally assumed I was an Israeli Jew and therefore someone who represented a threat to his form of life. So he leaned down to pick up a rock. And I knew he was going to throw it at me if I didn't turn around right away. All I could think to say was "mish Yehudi"—which means "I'm not Jewish" in Arabic. And strangely, this was enough. It was enough anyway to diffuse the situation and allow me to continue on my way home. But more importantly, it was enough to leave me with a vague appreciation that ours is a world that is shot through with differences that hang together, if at all, in a way that is surprisingly fragile. It is probably not unfair to say that my current efforts as an academic working in what we call theology and philosophy are an extension of my early efforts to make sense of this strange and confusing situation.

And yet there was also a sense in which I hated living in Jerusalem and couldn't wait to get back home to Winnipeg. But it was not because of the presence of war. I hated it because it meant that I didn't have access to the movies and new albums I knew my friends were enjoying back at home. I would get letters from friends telling me about the new Clash album or about this new movie called ET they had just seen and yet this only drove home the point that I was missing out. Things took a little longer to get from one side of the ocean to the other back in those days. Eventually, I found a record shop in West Jerusalem where I could buy my Clash albums. But by the time I got them, I knew my friends had already moved on to something else. And that was hard to take. I couldn't wait to move back home.

And when we finally did come home, it totally sucked. I ended up attending a private Mennonite high school called Westgate. It was a jarring experience of feeling out of place in a place that was supposed to feel like home. How much of that had to do with the fact that it was a Mennonite school or whether it was simply a kind of reverse culture shock of moving back from Jerusalem to Winnipeg is hard for me to say. But I distinctly remember an incident some time toward the beginning of the school year. I was walking down the hallway and overheard some of the girls talking with curiosity about the new Jewish kid. It made me curious too and I wondered why I hadn't met him yet. And then I realized they were talking about me. I didn't exactly mind that they thought I was Jewish. I was more put off by the ignorance reflected in their assumption that if you lived in Jerusalem you must be Jewish. I would eventually figure out a way to survive the social dynamics at Westgate. But I didn't exactly flourish academically or socially while I was there. I was interested in exploring other things that weren't part of the curriculum. But there was no equivalent to the Jerusalem Studies course and my inclination for exploring strange new territory did not seem to be suited to this new academic environment. Of course, I was also interested in pushing buttons testing the limits of authority. And it turns out I was quite good at that. But more than anything, I found the whole experience dull and uninteresting. There seemed to be no appreciation for the wandering, adventurous spirit that had been cultivated during my time in Jerusalem. Among other things, I took this to be a lesson that you should be careful what you wish for. Because you might actually get what you want. It was also an early appreciation of the reality that the problem with being Christian in North America is that it tends to be so damn boring. Again, it would take some time before I could put words to this experience. But when I went to study with Hauerwas and heard him talk about how the problem with Christianity in North America is that it has nothing worth dying for, it really resonated with me.

So what did I learn in Jerusalem? I learned that to be Christian is to be drawn into an adventure in which you are not in control of your own destiny. I came to appreciate how difficult it is to live truthfully and how important it is to avoid cultivating habits of self-deception. And I also came to appreciate that this effort is such that it is always to some degree bound to fail. But more than anything else, I think I learned something about the significance of what Christians refer to as the theological virtue of hope. By speaking of hope as a theological virtue, I mean to differentiate it from that sentimentalized version of Hollywood hope where we always eventually get what we wanted. I also mean to contrast it with the kind of hope that is typically equated with optimism. The theological conception of hope that was nourished in me when I lived in Jerusalem was also informed by the angry, punk-fueled critical spirit that I learned from Joe Strummer and the Clash and by the palpable sense of frustration that was present pretty much everywhere we went. This is a hope that isn't ever really satisfied. Or at least it is a hope that cannot be satisfied too easily. Of course, this also means that the lessons we learn are only ever partly learned. There is always a lot more learning to do. If Christianity is an adventure, it is one in which there is always more wandering to be done. Thanks be to God.

Chapter 6

The Perplexity of Ministry

Originally preached at Charleswood Mennonite Church, Winnipeg, MB
May 6, 2010, Ordination of Jeff Friesen
Scripture Texts: Isaiah 6:1-8; 2 Tim 4:1-5; Acts 6:1-7

> We whose profession it is to teach the inner meanings of religion
> find ourselves in perplexity. We may be hopeful but we cannot be
> happy. We darkly suspected when we were students that it would
> be so; we have grown older and it is worse than we suspected.
> Whether we are ministers in parishes or ministers in professional
> [university] chairs, it is always the same perplexity; none of us can
> avoid it. . . . Our perplexity comes to us simply and solely because
> we are ministers.
> -Karl Barth, *The Word of God and the Word of Man*, 183.

These words were spoken by the great Swiss theologian Karl Barth
in his reflections on the task of ministry. To be a minister, Barth
suggests, is to be confronted with a particular sort of perplexity—a
perplexity that leaves the task of ministry stained by a sense of
unhappiness. Why unhappiness? Because ministry is an endlessly
frustrating vocation. This is because the minister is charged with a task
that is quite literally impossible—to speak the word of God. So the
minister cannot be happy, if by happy we mean a sense of
accomplishment, of satisfaction in having achieved one's goals. If
ministry can be said to have a goal at all, it is a goal that is by definition
unattainable. As Barth puts it, "The task of the minister is the word of
God. This spells the certain defeat of the minister."[1] To be a minister is,
in other words, to embody failure.

Contemporary popular culture, it seems, is at least partly right on
this score. Think of how often the figure of the pastor functions in film

---

[1] Barth, *The Word of God and the Word of Man*, 214.

or television to represent an image of failure. Or how frequently we see the preacher presented as an unhappy and lonely figure. The most straightforward instance of this caricature is perhaps the profoundly apathetic character of Reverend Lovejoy from *The Simpsons*, who is referred to in one episode as "the priest who didn't care." But there are many others. And to be sure, there are also cases in which the minister is painted in a more positive light—usually as an inspiring role model or a figure that makes a positive difference of some sort. And sometimes they are even presented as being happy. But I think it is the caricature of ministry as a vocation for failures that is the more common image, at least in contemporary North America. It is surely the more interesting and challenging image to think about.

What sort of parent wishes for their children, upon graduation from high school or university, that they might aspire to a career in ministry? A doctor? Yes, please. A lawyer? Sure, why not? A research scientist? Maybe. But a minister? I suspect the parent would respond by saying something like, "Are you sure you've really thought this through?" Or perhaps, "Have you ever considered the possibility of becoming a teacher?" Why would anyone in their right mind intentionally pursue a career in ministry? This is simply not something parents and teachers encourage successful students to consider. If anything, it seems we think of ministry as a kind of last-ditch line of work that is reserved as a kind of respectable option for those kindhearted people of moderate intellectual ability who nevertheless lack a healthy sense of ambition. Is this popular conception of the ministry as a refuge for failures not at least partly the reason why so many ministers experience a sense of dread when the familiar game of making conversation with strangers leads to the inevitable question, "What it is that you do for a living?" Talk about a conversation stopper. Or at least a question that provokes a period of awkward stammering.

But if popular culture is right to see ministry as a kind of failure, it is nevertheless right for all the wrong reasons. The failure of the minister is not something that happens when ministry goes bad. It is, on the contrary, a mark of its success. The failed minister is not an exemplification of religion at its worst—something that is irrelevant at best and dangerously oppressive at worst, a relic left over from the so-called Dark Ages. Rather, it flows from an understanding of religion at its best. The failure of ministry arises from the fact that the minister is caught in a kind of double bind from which there is no way out: to speak of God is at once necessary and impossible. Once again, Barth sums it up nicely: "As ministers we ought to speak of God. We are human, however, and so cannot speak of God. We ought therefore to recognize both *our obligation and our inability* and by that very recognition give God the glory. This is our perplexity. The rest of our task fades into insignificance in comparison."[2]

This is arguably one of the most critical features of the Christian tradition. Call it the tension between the cataphatic and apophatic, of positive and negative speech about God. And yet it is also a feature that is apparently one of the easiest to forget. Think of all the contemporary Christians who speak as if they have a complete grasp on the word of God. This is the sort of approach that popular culture mocks with its portrayals of the failed Christian minister. From Barth's perspective, this is to miss the forest for the trees. It was Augustine who summarized this tension-filled logic of Christianity most succinctly, presenting it as a rule that might be said to inform meaningful speech about God: "If you understand it, then it is not God." God is not an object about which we can claim a kind of positive knowledge. Rather, God is a mystery with whom we are called to be in relation. And the task of the minister is to orient us to this mystery. Not by making vague pronouncements about the ineffable. But rather, by offering specific descriptions of the Christian life, each of which is somehow inadequate if taken on its own terms.

If you understand it, then it is not God. To speak of God is at once necessary, but impossible. This understanding of Christianity lies at the heart of Marilynne Robinson's recent novel, *Gilead*, which is surely one of the great literary portrayals of the task of ministry. Robinson is not only one of the finest living novelists writing in English. She is also herself an astute reader of Barth. *Gilead* is a novel that takes the form of a series of letters written by an aging minister to his young son. It is a story about fathers and sons, about failure and forgiveness, about life lived in the shadow of death. But it is really a story about a kind of humble yet profound wisdom that can emerge when one embraces the kind of perplexity that Barth points to. In one of his letters, the old Reverend complains about those who assume that his primary task is to convince a skeptical generation to believe in God. "[T]hey want me to defend religion, and they want me to give them 'proofs.' But I just won't

---

[2] Ibid., 186.

do it. It only confirms them in their skepticism. Because nothing true can be said about God from a posture of defense. . . . So my advice is this—don't look for proofs. Don't bother with them at all. They are never sufficient to the question, and they're always a little impertinent, I think, because they claim for God a place within our conceptual grasp."[3]

It is important to recognize that Barth says it is *through* the recognition of her or his inability to speak the word of God that the minister gives God the glory. Inability here is not presented as something we must seek to overcome, like a bad habit. If the perplexity of ministry names a kind of double bind, it is not a tragic one, whereby the minister is trapped in a situation from which no good can possibly come. Rather, Barth, Augustine, and Robinson are all giving expression to a comedic vision in which the good comes to us in surprising ways, as a gift we did not expect to receive. It happens to us, not because of our efforts let alone our credentials, but in spite of them. And so the double bind of ministry is not to be thought of as a temporary weakness from which we might one day escape. Rather, the minister is charged with the task of calling into question the assumption that we should be looking for a way out, that we can find a way to avoid failure if only we were smart enough and applied our smarts with single-minded dedication. The task of ministry is to embody this double bind. The good minister does not seek to avoid or even minimize failure, but embraces it and follows it all the way through to the other side. We might even say that the minister is one who is skilled in the arts of productive failure. Among other things, this suggests that ministry is an entirely different sort of work than other forms of work. To assume that the vocation of ministry can be compared straightforwardly with other vocations is to commit a category mistake. A good minister is one who recognizes this, and in so doing gives concrete expression to the perplexity of ministry.

I suspect that, more often than not, ministry is not something that is intentionally chosen as a vocation, at least not the way high school students show up at university with a sense of a career plan they are ready to embark on. The call to ministry is, rather, something that happens. It catches us entirely by surprise, even as we may eventually come to embrace it with a sense of confidence. This is what the Christian tradition means by speaking of it in the language of calling. To be called is to be given a task that we would not have chosen on our own. It is a

---

[3] Robinson, *Gilead*, 177.

task that probably does not make a whole lot of sense. But then the Bible is full of stories of a God who seems to specialize in catching us off guard.

Is this not what is reflected in the passage from Isaiah that Jeff chose as one of our Scripture texts this morning? "Woe is me! I am lost, for I am a man of unclean lips, and I live among a people of unclean lips; yet my eyes have seen the King, the Lord of hosts!" (Isa 6:5) This is the person who was chosen to speak the word of God. And in what did the speech of the one so chosen consist? Isaiah continues where our text left off by telling us what the voice of the Lord instructed this chosen one to say: "Keep listening, but do not comprehend; keep looking, but do not understand. Make the mind of this people dull, and stop their ears, and shut their eyes, so that they may not look with their eyes, and listen with their ears, and comprehend with their minds, and turn and be healed." (Isa 6:9-10) If you understand, it is not God. To speak of God is at once necessary and impossible.

I am sure that Jeff is able to relate to this sense of the perplexity of ministry—and not only because we studied Barth together in a seminar I offered at CMU a couple of years ago. But this sermon is not finally about Jeff. It is about the strange sort of phenomenon that is ordination to Christian ministry. On the one hand, ordination can be said to reflect a sense of confidence. We as a church—both locally and more broadly—are affirming Jeff's call to be a minister of the church. It is an affirmation of his gifts and a declaration of trust in his ability to provide leadership for us. On the other hand, beneath this confidence runs an undercurrent of confusion about the role and value of ministry. It is one of those things we do in the church and yet don't really understand why we do it. But perhaps this is okay. Maybe it is even as it should be.

I want to end by returning our attention to the question of happiness. Barth suggests that ministry is marked by a sense of unhappiness. But he is really suggesting that what we call happiness is transformed by the God who claims us as his people. This transformed happiness is not first of all about reaching goals or feeling content. It is not a name for what we like most about ourselves. Rather, it is a happiness that comes from the recognition that God is not ours to understand. God is profoundly different, radically other. This kind of happiness is not exactly of the world. But in a world of rabid narcissism, it is a life-giving breath of fresh air. It is this kind of happiness that I have sensed in Jeff's work among us in the last number of years. And I wish him more of this happiness as he continues in his ministry.

Chapter 7

When Valentine's Day and Ash Wednesday Collide

Originally offered as a chapel reflection at CMU
Feb. 14, 2018, Ash Wednesday
Scripture Texts: Psalm 51; Matthew 6:1-5, 16-20.

Today is Ash Wednesday. It is also the feast day of St Valentine, which is more commonly referred to these days as Valentine's Day. Given that the dating of their occurrence is based on two different calendar systems, the coincidence of these two special days is rather unusual. The last time Ash Wednesday fell on Valentine's Day was in 1945. It will happen a couple more times in the coming years—in 2024 and then again in 2029. But after that, it will be another 121 years before Ash Wednesday coincides with Valentine's Day. So like everyone else who has been asked to preach on this day, I'm going to take the bait and reflect a little bit on what to make of this unusual twist of calendrical fate.

Let me begin by rehearsing what might be called the standard approaches to this convergence. I note at the outset that each of them begins by noting an apparent tension if not outright contradiction between the two days. The only question, then, is how to go about resolving it. For some, the tension between the two days is so significant that they simply cannot occupy the same space. By appealing to Christian liturgical practices, many go on to argue that Ash Wednesday should displace Valentine's Day from the spot on the calendar it usually occupies. For example, the American Catholic Bishop Richard Malone reminded his parishioners in Buffalo that "Ash Wednesday and Good Friday are the only two days of the whole year on which fasting and abstinence are required." He went on to suggest that "[t]hose who are accustomed to celebrating Valentine's Day might do so the day before.

Join it up with Mardis Gras."[1] Notice how this approach places the emphasis on practice. Since the practices of fasting and abstinence are duties we are called to perform on Ash Wednesday, it follows that the sort of feasting that might otherwise be practiced on Valentine's Day is not allowed this year. Note also that the feasting associated with Valentine's Day is not absolutely prohibited by such an approach. There are legitimately festive times and then there are times for fasting. Bishop Malone is simply stating that what might otherwise be permissible on Mardi Gras or Valentine's Day has no place on Ash Wednesday. There are no doubt others who would argue that it should be the other way around, that Valentine's Day festivities should trump the austere practices of Ash Wednesday. But these accounts tend not to be theologically informed in any sort of meaningful way. So I'll leave it up to you to imagine how this approach might play itself out.

For others, the tension is less a matter of respecting the strict hierarchy of liturgical practices and more a question about the meaning or spirit that is thought to lie behind those practices. Here we tend to find the coincidence of the two days approached not so much as a zero-sum conflict that can only be overcome by tilting the balance to one side or the other, but rather as a welcome opportunity to provide some much needed nuance and clarification to a rather crude conception of love that has come to be associated with Valentine's Day. Here, it is argued that whatever love Christians celebrate on Valentine's Day, it should be consistent with the sort of posture associated with Ash Wednesday. Cardinal Timothy Dolan, the Archbishop of New York, endorses such an approach when he advises his parishioners that "Valentine's Day celebrations of love are permitted so long as they are in line with the spirit of Ash Wednesday."[2] Ash Wednesday, in other words, is presented as an occasion to understand the *real* meaning of the love celebrated on Valentine's Day, an opportunity to purge it of its worldly or secular perversions. Another such account from the Marian Catholic tradition stresses that "love inevitably requires sacrifice." After noting a stark decline in marriage rates, the author elaborates by saying: "True love does not depend upon our changing emotions, but on choosing to sacrifice for others. These choices may not give us the greatest feelings. In fact, sometimes we have to act against how we feel for the sake of

---

[1] Quoted in Sharon Otterman, "Eat, Pray, Love: An Ash Wednesday and Valentine's Day Dilemma," *New York Times*, February 12, 2018.

[2] Otterman, "Eat, Pray, Love."

love. When we do, we may suffer, but through this pain the Lord promises that we will find peace."[3] On such a reading, the love celebrated on Valentine's Day should *always* be the sort of self-sacrificial love to which we are pointed on Ash Wednesday. So there is really no conflict, just misunderstanding. The tension between Valentine's Day and Ash Wednesday is not so much resolved as it is dissolved. There was only ever an apparent conflict, not a real one.

This approach is bolstered by the suggestion that Valentine's Day is a distortion of the original spirit of St Valentine. Here, the main point is that St Valentine never really had anything to do with love in the first place. On the contrary, we are told that Valentine's Day came to be associated with courtly love by Geoffrey Chaucer and that it only came to be associated with the contemporary notion of romantic love in and around the 19th Century. So whatever it is that Valentine's Day has become for us, it is a distortion of the story of the early Christian martyr named Valentinus. And hence the tension can be dissolved by ditching Valentine's Day and reinstituting the original feast day of Saint Valentine.[4]

Now, I have to confess I don't really find any of these accounts terribly compelling. Without elaborating, I suspect this is because I find in each of them a rather crude association of Christian love and self-sacrifice. By contrast, I'm more inclined to follow the atheist French Philosopher Alain Badiou and the American Catholic Cardinal Joseph Tobin, strange bedfellows to be sure. Let me simply leave you with two quotes, one about love and the other about Ash Wednesday. Reflecting on the writings of St Paul, Badiou claims that any conception of love "which claims that the subject annihilates himself in a direct relationship to the transcendence of the Other is nothing more than narcissistic pretention."[5] This posture of self-sacrifice is not love, he claims, but rather a false simulacrum of love. Cardinal Tobin makes a similar claim about narcissistic temptations that can be found in certain conceptions of Ash Wednesday. He summarizes the passage from Matthew that we heard this morning with the following advice: "You can be happy and

---

[3] Massery, "Love Requires Sacrifice," *The Divine Mercy* (website), posted February 13, 2018. https://www.thedivinemercy.org/news/Valentines-Day-is-Ash-Wednesday-What-to-Make-of-That-7535

[4] See Massery, "Love Requires Sacrifice."

[5] Badiou, *St Paul*, 90.

enjoy the day, and you certainly shouldn't be dour, because then all the attention is on you, on your discomfort."[6]

Another difficulty I have with the so-called standard approaches is that they seem to presume that these discourses of love and death somehow demand to be reconciled. I suspect, however, that they can't be. At least not in any neat sort of way that might count as an explanation. What if the impulse to love and the reality of death are somehow both unavoidable and yet irreconcilable aspects of what it means to be human, to be a creature? Here the problem is not so much with the tension between love and death. It is the desire to resolve the tension, to explain it away, that is problematic. What if the truth is messier and more complicated than our desire for explanation allows? At any rate, let me confess my preference for lingering with the difficulty of these messier accounts rather than seeking the explanations of those who strive for a sort of conceptual neatness.

Speaking of messy accounts, please indulge me as I conclude by drawing attention to another story that forces its way into my own reckoning with this day, namely the death of the disgraced Italian cycling legend Marco Pantani. The story of Pantani is shot through with traces of all the themes we've discussed so far, albeit in a non-linear and distinctly tragic sort of way. I doubt that anybody would suggest that Pantani should find himself considered alongside Valentinus as a saint. There are some, however, who take him to be a martyr. Let me just say, without getting into it, that they are wrong, and that their error is less about the details of Pantani's life and more about the concept of martyrdom. At any rate, I approach Pantani as something more along the lines of a tortured, negative exemplar one might find on a pilgrimage through the world of the dead like that which we find in Dante's *Divine Comedy*. With the question of Ash Wednesday in mind, it is interesting to note that in his later years Pantani had a habit of marking his mountaintop victories with a posture that can only be described as cruciform. And while it's not unfair to describe him as a romantic of sorts, it also needs to be acknowledged that his love life was nothing short of a mess. And so it is not without some irony that his life came to an end on Valentine's Day in 2004.

Five days earlier, he'd checked himself into a hotel on the Adriatic coast of Italy, just south of Ravenna, where Dante also spent the latter

---

[6] Otterman, "Eat, Pray, Love."

part of his life after he was exiled from Florence. In one of many tragic twists of fate that mark the story of Pantani's life, the name of the hotel was The Rose. What happened during those five days is not entirely clear, in part because Pantani was no longer communicating with anyone. But there is no doubt that it involved a toxic mix of cocaine, mental illness, and a failure to come to grips with a life outside of cycling that had been building ever since he was disqualified from the 1999 Tour of Italy—a race he was poised to win—for "abnormal blood values." At the end of his searing biography on Pantani, which I've just finished reading again, as I often do in the days leading up to Valentine's Day, Matt Rendell suggests that "[t]he idea of sport Marco embodied wasn't one that encouraged athletes to face the truth about their existence."[7] This is, as Rendell recognizes, not just limited to sport. Rather, this conception of the athletic life is but a part of "a generalized culture of deception."[8] And perhaps more than any of his impressive achievements and skills in cycling, it is arguably this culture of deception that best describes the context in which Pantani was a virtuoso. At any rate, Rendell suggests that it was his narcissistic capacity for self-deception that, in the end, cost him his life. What does any of this have to do with Valentine's Day and Ash Wednesday? On the one hand, nothing. It is surely just another tragic twist of fate that Pantani's life came to an end on Valentine's Day. And this year, the contingencies of time invite us to consider his life in relation to the question of Ash Wednesday as well. On the other hand, if the comments by Alain Badiou and Cardinal Tobin come anywhere close to the truth, there may be a way of connecting the dots. But I'd prefer to leave the dots in place and invite us to linger amongst them for a little while.

I've spoken about this year's occurrence of Valentine's Day and Ash Wednesday as a coincidence. But perhaps it is better to think of it as something more like a collision. Pantani's life was full of violent collisions—on the bike, in cars, and in any number of other encounters. What if the coming together of Valentine's Day and Ash Wednesday is less a coincidence and more like a collision that happens when both Valentine's Day and Ash Wednesday are approached in pious ways that shield us from the need to confront our own temptations toward self-deception?

---

[7] Rendell, *The Death of Marco Pantani*, 291-292.
[8] Ibid., 292.

My youngest son is named Marcus. He wasn't named after Marco Pantani. But like Pantani, Marcus likes to race his bike. And he loves to dominate races, an experience I cannot say I've ever had. I confess that in my weaker moments, it's far too easy to wish Marcus the sort of success that Pantani found in his better days as a cyclist. But in my more sober moments, I pray that he will be spared the tragedy that results from the forms of self-deception Pantani embodied. That he might be able to navigate the darkness without being consumed by it. Happy Valentine's Day, Marcus. Remember that you are dust, and to dust you shall return.

Chapter 8

What Are You Afraid Of?
Lenten Reflections on the Eve of War

Originally offered as a chapel reflection at CMU
March 17, 2003, three days before the American-led invasion of Iraq
Scripture Text: Psalm 111: 1-10; Luke 12:4-7

In Lent we are often told to leave our fear behind. Put your faith in God alone and you will have nothing to fear. It is a comforting message of assurance and security. It is also a true message, but only a half-truth at best. We have all heard the message before. Indeed, I suspect that we've heard it so often that we are a bit numb to the full significance of its meaning. Let us leave our fear behind. In the end, everything will be alright. To be given the promise that fear can be overcome is indeed comforting. None of us finds comfort in fear! At least not in the kind of bone-rattling and mind-numbing genuine fear that paralyses and debilitates. Such fear can bring life to a standstill even as we go on living. It is the sort of thing that brings us close to the world of zombies, the living dead. The idea of leaving fear behind is a most appealing prospect. It is at the heart of the contemporary Christian therapy industry. And it is attractive because it promises to be empowering. It holds out the possibility of being released from paralysis and continuing to go about the business of living our lives. And this is a message we all want to hear. But that is exactly why such a promise deserves more careful scrutiny.

Take, for example, Ned Flanders from *The Simpsons*. In our lust for comfort we are often pointed in a direction that causes us to miss the heart of the gospel message. In the case of Flanders, we are presented with a version of sentimentalized Christianity that misses the sense in which the Christian life might be described as inherently difficult. Let us take another look at the Scripture passage that was read for us this morning. Jesus says, "I tell you my friends, do not fear those who kill the body, and after that have no more that they can do. But I will warn you whom to fear: fear him who, after he has killed, has the power to cast you into hell; yes, I tell you, fear him!" (Luke 12:4-5) I don't know about you, but as I read these words I am almost naturally tempted to concentrate on the first half of what Jesus says. This is the comforting and consoling half; the part of the gospel message that assures us that our fears will be overcome, that they can safely be left behind. But we would miss the message if we failed to notice the other half of what Jesus says. He does not stop with the message of therapeutic comfort. He does not simply do away with fear. On the contrary, we might say that he ups the ante. He redirects our fear, and reminds us that there is a more profound kind of fear to be had, namely fear of God. To fear God is not merely to fear death. It is to fear not only that which can kill you, but to fear the one who has the power to cast you into hell. When we read the whole thing, including the parts that we really don't want to read, the passage turns out not really to be about leaving fear behind at all. Rather, it is about having our fears redirected and transformed. It is a message which suggests that the Christian life involves training in what we might call having the right kinds of fear. It is not, in other words, a question of whether or not we fear. Rather, the question is "what are we afraid of?"

So what are you afraid of? I'm afraid of lightning. Like all genuine fears, there is a story behind this one. I won't go into all the embarrassing details here. But this story took place at the Hecla Island Golf Course. I believe it was at the tee-off box to the sixth hole. We had seen the storm approaching, and I had already lobbied for the group to abandon the game and go back to the clubhouse. But this was a group of Mennonite golfers and we had paid good money to take our hacks. There would be no turning back. For a while it looked like the storm might abate, that we would be spared. But at the end of the fifth hole, the dark clouds returned and the flashes of lightning began to pop. Then the clouds opened up and we were pelted by wave after wave of rain. Since there was no rain shelter in sight, we huddled against the wooden sign containing the map of the hole and all the relevant details that a better golfer might actually attempt to incorporate into his game. And it started to rain harder and harder. And the pops turned into canon-like explosions, until—and I can still see this as clearly and distinctly as I did the moment it happened—a bolt of lightning struck a tree directly across the fairway from where we were standing. Under a tree. Where is the one place you are taught not to hide in a lightning storm? That's exactly where we were. Huddled under a tree. The combination of fear and absurdity was too much for me to bear. The clap of thunder was louder than anything I'd ever heard before. To call it a clap is hardly to do it justice. Claps are happy sounds. This was a fierce and terrifying roar. And the other thing about it is there was no delay. The sound arrived simultaneously with the vision of the lightning strike itself, slicing the thick humid air just as it struck more fear in my already terrified body. This means, of course, that the lightning strike was very, very close. Which is not exactly something I needed confirmed for me. So it only made things worse. The tree disintegrated right in front of us. All I could think to do was run. Actually, "think" is not exactly the right word to use, because as I began to think again, while I was running across the fairway, I realized that running was a futile and stupid response. There was no good place to hide. I was convinced I was going to die. The only way to describe the experience is to speak of paralysis. I was running as fast as I could, yet I was completely paralyzed. And I am often still paralysed by fear when I hear lightning approach, even though I'm getting better at disguising it for the sake of my children.

Against the background of these sorts of experiences, let me differentiate between two ways of reading what Jesus has to say about fear. One way—call it the comforting way—says that fears such as the fear of lightning are nothing to be afraid of. At the very most, it can kill you. No big deal. The Christian life is bigger than the life of the body, let alone any individual body. Another way of reading it suggests that fear of lightning is really a kind of pseudo-fear. It is to have our fears misdirected. It is to be afraid of the wrong sorts of things. It is to be preoccupied with death, or rather our inability to control death, whereas God is beyond the question of life and death. To call us to have our fears redirected to God is to call us to a new way of life—a life which trades not in violence and death, but rather exists as an ongoing non-violent exchange of giving and receiving.

I suspect we have a hard time knowing what it means to be afraid of God. It is tempting to suggest that this is a distinctly modern phenomenon, as we contemporary Christians struggle with what it means to be Christian even as we are complicit in the death of the very God we claim to worship. But to go down that road is to miss the point of the passage. The difficulty we have in knowing what it means to fear God was shared by the people to whom Jesus spoke. So what did he say to them? He did not counsel them to leave their fears behind. To suggest that fear can be left behind is to provide a message of security. This is the kind of thing one could imagine being uttered in the halls of government in the aftermath of the attacks of September 11, 2001 and the wider phenomenon of terrorism. Don't let fear consume you; keep spending. To suggest that fear can be left behind is to suggest that fear can be policed and God is the great police officer. That kind of fear works because it trades on disrupting that which we think we can control. That is a kind of fear, but it is not the kind of fear that is captured by speaking of the fear of God. To speak against this kind of fear, as Jesus did, is to challenge the temptation to mastery and control in the first place. To be afraid of God is to move beyond a preoccupation with security. It is to recognize that the Christian life is not a possession over which we are in control, but names a life of dispossession. To be afraid of God is to have our fears reoriented such that we give up the temptation to be in control. It names a way of life where the stranger is not named as a threat against which we must protect ourselves, but rather welcomed, as the parable of the Good Samaritan illustrates. Not only welcomed, but welcomed in a way that we become vulnerable to the stranger, to the other, to the Other that is God. Jesus calls us to leave behind the fear of death, not because death is a minor inconvenience in comparison to what awaits us after we die. Rather, he calls us to leave behind the fear of death, because to be afraid of death is but another way of saying that what we really worship is ourselves. Instead he calls us to fear God. And this is not so much a comforting message, as a message that the self is exactly what will have to be given up in following Christ.

To speak of the fear of God in this way is to try and take to heart what Rowan Williams calls "the most central and disturbing and genuinely *theological* question we could ask: 'How do I know it's *God* I'm talking about?'"[1] Elsewhere, Williams suggests that "Language about God is kept honest in the degree to which it turns on itself in the name of God, and so surrenders itself to God: it is in this way that it becomes possible to see how it is still *God* that is being spoken of, that which makes the human world a moral unity."[2] I am suggesting that we should understand the question of the fear of God as another way of getting at the same basic concern that drives the enterprise of theology in the first place, namely the question of idolatry. Am I fearing the right things? Is it really God I'm talking about? These are pertinent questions in all times

---

[1] Williams, *A Ray of Darkness*, 243.
[2] Williams, "Theological Integrity," 8.

and places. But I think these words ring forth with a kind of weighty resonance as we are perched on the eve of war. Is it God I am speaking of? Are we confusing being Christian with being American or Canadian? When President Bush enlists God in support of the war on terrorism or the impending war on Iraq, is he speaking of the Christian God? Williams goes on to suggest that "the challenge for the theologian, pastor, or preacher, indeed for every even faintly articulate Christian, is to find a [form of] speech that allows this question to be heard—not as a moment of corrosive doubt or comfortable uncertainty, but as a kind of confessional pointing to the truth that can reconstitute our words and our human bonds."[3]

Remember that what we are practising here is Lent. Lent is a time of putting our faith into proper perspective. It is a time of acknowledging the strangeness of God and our status as creatures who have been called into being by that strange God. In this respect, it is about training; about being initiated and transformed into a new way of seeing and being in the world. It is not a question of whether or not to have fear in the first place. Rather, the question is "What are you afraid of?" This formation of what we might call Christian fear is what we are practising during Lent. Having the right sorts of fears and having them be experienced in the right manner. It is fitting to close with the words of Psalm 111:10: "The fear of the Lord is the beginning of wisdom; all those who practice it have a good understanding. His praise endures forever."

---

[3] Williams, *A Ray of Darkness*, 244.

Chapter 9

The Gift of Lent: On Lent and Self-Denial

Originally preached at Home Street Mennonite Church, Winnipeg, MB
March 15, 2015, fourth Sunday of Lent
Scripture Texts: Psalm107:1-3, 17-22; Ephesians 2:1-10

It is the fourth Sunday of Lent—a wonderfully complicated time of the Christian calendar. I suspect most of us tend to think of Lent as an exercise in self-sacrifice or self-denial. Lent is penitential time, a time for confession, conversion, and curbing temptation. It is, in other words, a period of time during which we strive to perfect the Christian art of renunciation. There seems to be a pretty standard template for how to go about this. Identify a particular bad habit or guilty pleasure that you know you are probably better off doing without. And see if you can survive without giving into it for six weeks. Typically, this form of renunciation is associated with the act of giving something up. What we renounce is our desire for some particular thing or range of things. More than once in the past few weeks, I've overheard conversations in the hallways at CMU that start with someone asking, "So, what are you giving up for Lent this year?" Or, perhaps less presumptuously, "Are you giving anything up for Lent this year?" And of course in our market driven world of information management, there are even polls and market research dedicated to providing data on the answers that people give to these sorts of questions. I recently heard a radio report on CBC—by a business reporter, no less—who was reporting on a new study that found, among Christians who give up something for Lent, that a growing number of them are giving up some form of technology. I'm not sure what is stranger here: that there are some people who think this is the sort of information that must be gathered and quantified in the first place or that this data is especially newsworthy for the business world. This strikes me as a strange inversion of the kind of commercial significance typically associated with Christmas. If there is news here, it's because of what Christians are *not* buying or consuming. In any case, by technology, the study meant things like smart phones and tablets, texting and social networks, television and video games. My 13 year old daughter was also in the car and rightly noted the carelessness of the report, pointing out that technology includes things like forks and spoons, clothes and shoes too, which makes the whole idea of giving up technology for Lent sound kind of ridiculous, at least to a 13 year old. "Nobody would give up clothes for Lent," she said. "That's just stupid." But stupid or not, the point of the example is that it illustrates a particular way in which the popular Christian imagination associates Lent with a particular image of self-denial and renunciation. Self-denial, in this case, is equated with giving something up. Whether texting or television, or more traditional candidates like coffee or chocolate, Lent is an exercise of letting something go. It is to deny ourselves of something we normally desire. Moreover, Lenten discipline is thought to be at its most real when we let go of things we tend to hold on to rather tightly. It seems Lent is an opportunity to test our resolve, to work on strengthening our capacity for discipline and self-control. The work of self-denial is definitely a part of Lent. But is it the whole part? Or rather, is this the best way to understand what is meant by self-denial? The Scripture readings we've been given this morning seem to speak to precisely these questions.

As I read the Scripture texts for this morning's service, I'm struck by the relative absence of this way of thinking about self-denial as an exercise of giving something up. Instead, the emphasis seems to be on what we receive. Consider the passage from Psalm 107. The theme here is healing and deliverance and the appropriate sort of response that is called for when these things happen, namely "thanksgiving sacrifices" and sharing the good news by singing "songs of joy." This passage does not suggest a program about what we are to give up. Rather the stress is on what we are given by God. Put differently, it is not what anyone does that seems to be of interest here. The passage speaks rather about what is done to us. Perhaps most significantly, it suggests that deliverance is not earned. It is a gift one is called to receive with an appropriate posture of humility and thanksgiving by way of return. The biblical word for such a response is "sacrifice"—a counter-gift whereby we give something to God.

These themes are stated even more forcefully in Paul's letter to the Ephesians. Paul is not one to mince words. His style is not what we might call "seeker-sensitive." If anything, it is offensive. He starts by calling out his audience—the church in Ephesus—and taking them to task, telling them that they are "dead through the trespasses and sins in which you once lived." (Eph. 2:1-2) They are dead, in other words, because they approach their lives as if it is *their* work—their lives—that matters. Paul stresses that this is not the way to approach Christ. Indeed, he suggests that Christ is, in some sense, not really to be approached at all. Rather, he comes to us. Or even better, he draws us in, pulls us into his love. As Dante so beautifully puts it in the *Divine Comedy*, Christ is like a lover wooing his beloved. It is for this reason that the church is traditionally referred to as the bride of Christ and conversion is narrated as a form of betrothal. Paul's word for all this is "grace." And the posture appropriate for those of us who are being wooed is called "faith." But notice also that Paul does not simply reject work or the active life and replace it with a passive conception of grace or faith. Rather, he suggests that faith changes the equation or turns things inside-out: we are "created in Christ Jesus for good works." (Eph. 2:10) Or as another translation puts it, in Christ we become the "workmanship of God." We might even say that we become the very gift of God through which grace and love radiate.

Paul's tone here is often called apocalyptic. He raises the stakes pretty high. But it is important to notice that his logic is the same as that of the Psalms. Through Christ we are saved from death and are given life. Elsewhere he speaks of this gift as a "new creation." We find here the same emphasis on giving, receiving, and thanksgiving that we found in Psalm 107. Only here the gift might be described as something more like life itself. Please note that Paul does not say that life is *a* gift. That is grammatically incorrect in a subtle but significant way. It implies that we are somehow already there ready to receive the gift. The biblical formula from Genesis through the Psalms to Paul is different in that it suggests life itself is gift. The gift, we might say, goes all the way down. Paul is suggesting that there is a world of difference between the logic of gift and the logic of ownership or possession. Among other things, this means that we are most truly alive when we acknowledge that our lives are not our own. Paul is calling the church in Ephesus—and, by extension, us—to live in such a way that we give up the illusion of being in control.

If these are Lenten passages, then they seem to suggest that Lent is less about giving up and more about learning how to receive gifts. Or perhaps a better way to put it is to say that Lent is more than a simple matter of a self that gives up some*thing*. Indeed, some practices of renunciation can be expressions of just the sort of self-righteous spirit of ownership and possession that the biblical language of gift sets out to correct. Denial, in other words, can all too easily become another form of self-assertion. We seem all too ready to boast of our ability to give up soda pop or social media. And to do so is to fall prey to exactly the sort of misunderstanding about which Paul warned the Ephesians. Or, to put it somewhat differently, think of how easy it is to approach the task of giving up in terms of a posture that assumes we must remain in control. I am the one who lets go of the things I once claimed as my own. Notice how this leaves me in a position of sovereignty over that which I relinquish. But the gist of these passages seems to cut in precisely the opposite direction. They are not first of all concerned with what is given up. Rather, they direct us to consider what we might call the work of receiving. And what do we receive? We receive a new kind of life. Most importantly, we receive a life that is structured by the giving and receiving of gifts rather than the structures of ownership, possession, and control. It is not just a question of what sorts of gifts we receive in our various lives. Life is gift. Our lives are not ours to control. We receive them from God.

It is in this sense that we are to understand Paul's well-known contrast between the flesh and the spirit, which also makes an appearance in the passage we were given to read this morning. In the grammar of the Bible, flesh and spirit do not name two different types of stuff, two different kinds of reality. They are not two different parts that come together to constitute a whole we call a whole human life. That is the way modern philosophy speaks of life—as a combination of body and mind. But in the biblical imagination flesh and spirit are better understood as forms of desire or ways of being. And they both refer to the whole of life. For Paul, flesh names a way of being that is structured by the habits of possession and ownership—a form of desire that is turned back in on itself. Spirit, by contrast, names a way of being that is structured as an exchange of giving and receiving. There is a reason we speak of the gift of the spirit as something that cannot be contained or controlled. The point is not a metaphysical claim that the spirit is immaterial or somehow other than bodily. The question is, rather, what the body looks like or how it moves. Does it move like the body Paul highlights for the Ephesians, like one whose life is received as gift? Or does it move like someone who is gripped by a desire for possession and ownership, a desire to be in control?

So now we get to the punchline. All of this takes us right back to the question of self-denial and renunciation, but with a significantly different twist. In light of these texts, it is hard to think of Lent as being just about giving up certain things and the bad habits that direct us toward them. They suggest a much larger notion of renunciation—a renunciation of a certain conception of the self. Just as gift goes all the way down, so does the practice of self-renunciation. Just as the Bible speaks not of a life, a self, that is there to receive a gift, so there is no self that is capable of letting things go. If anything, it is this very image of self that is being let go of here.

If this is right, then Lent is perhaps not so much a drama about a self that sacrifices something. Rather it's a drama in which it is the self that is sacrificed. It is a period in which we work intensely at acknowledging that our lives are not ours to control. Or, to put it in the language of Paul and the Psalms, it is a period in which we strive to work out what it means to appreciate that life is gift. This is why the traditional conception of Lent stresses almsgiving and charity as much as it does renunciation and self-denial. To give up a life of possessive ownership is to be drawn into a life of charitable sharing—less giving up than giving away, we might say. Or, it is ultimately about giving ourselves back to the God from whom we came. We seem to have lost sight of this in our contemporary discourse about Lent. But our texts this morning seem to be pointing to this larger imagination of Lenten discipline. Thanks be to God.

Chapter 10

Putting Ourselves in Question: The Triumphal Entry and the Renunciation of Triumphalism[1]

Originally preached at Hope Mennonite Church, Winnipeg, MB
April 13, 2003, Palm Sunday
Scripture Texts: Psalm 118:1-2; 19-29; Mark 11:1-11; Philippians 2:5-11

What is striking about the lectionary texts we have read this morning is the recurrent theme of unexpectedness, of strangeness, of mystery. The psalmist tells us that "the stone that the builders rejected has become the chief cornerstone." (Psalm 118: 22) This is to say that the wisdom of God is associated with that which flows against the stream. It consists of that which has been dismissed by those who are normally considered to be wise. It flies in the face of received opinions and disturbs what we customarily refer to as common sense. Mark's account of Jesus's triumphal entry into Jerusalem is destabilizing at its very core with its central image of Jesus riding into town on a lowly donkey. The arrival of Jesus, the one who has been proclaimed king, is thus a rejection of the usual mechanisms of kingship. The triumphal entry, we might say, involves the renunciation of triumphalism. This theme is echoed, perhaps even intensified, by Paul. In his letter to the Philippians, Paul writes that the lordship of Christ is not that of one who rules by domination and might. It does not resemble what he elsewhere calls the powers. Rather, we are reminded that Jesus emptied himself, became humble, and took the form of a servant. Unlike other rulers, Jesus does not rule by deploying brute force. He does not rule by wielding power, but by taking the form of a servant. To model our lives after Jesus, as Paul is calling us to do, is thus to have our lives radically changed. It is far more than just being given a second chance. It is to be remade, as we

---

are inscribed into a fundamentally different *kind* of life. To confess that Jesus Christ is Lord, as Paul calls us to, is to have our lives transformed on the basis of a redefined model of lordship. To confess that Jesus is the master is to begin to participate in a way of life that renounces mastery. It is to embark on the hard journey of learning how to give up the temptation to be in control.

What is noteworthy about each of these readings is that they repeat a pattern that is fundamentally disruptive. Each might be said to involve a way of putting ourselves in question. They disturb many of our central convictions and upset the exceedingly comfortable character of our lives. They challenge the assumptions we hold dear and unsettle the boundaries and territorial schemes of order we erect to protect ourselves and to exclude those others we deem threatening. All of which is to say that they are profoundly mysterious in the sense that they transcend what it is that we can grasp with our knowledge. Paul tells us to have among us the mind of Jesus Christ. This is to remind us that we will not be saved by the contents of our own or anyone else's mind. The story of Jesus Christ is not something that we could possibly have come up with on our own. Paul's concern is not with the content of our minds— with what we might call our knowledge claims—but rather their form. His point is that our minds are in need of transformation and reordering. Some speak of this as participating in the mind of Jesus Christ. This is what I take Paul to mean when he says "let the same mind be in you that was in Christ Jesus." (Phil. 2:5)

Not only does this include the redefinition of what counts as knowledge, it challenges the assumption that knowledge involves always having to say something new. To say that the mind of Christ, the wisdom of God, is mysterious is to say that there are some matters which are not up to us to settle and determine. There are some things, in other words, whose business it is not ours to resolve. Our task is not to make everything come out right. Our goal is not to ensure that things turn out the way we think they ought to be. Rather, it is to have the nature of our thoughts and our oughts rethought. One of Paul's central messages is the reminder that life is gift. As such, it comes unexpectedly, undeservedly, and unnecessarily. Moreover, its very nature as gift means that it is cancelled out when it is turned into something we possess and over which we claim to exercise control. We are called to live a life of gift-exchange with others, which means that we are called to become vulnerable to one another. And so the temptation to settle is itself unsettled.

Today we make the transition from Lent into Holy Week. It is the climax of the Christian year. It is a time when we celebrate and are confronted with what it means to participate in the life, death, and resurrection of Christ. Having been prepared by going through the Lenten exercise of surrendering that in which we falsely put our hopes, this is a time when we are brought face to face with the implications of reconsidering much of what we have come to hold dear. Indeed, this is a time when time itself is redefined. "This is the day that the Lord has made; let us rejoice and be glad in it," the Psalmist tells us. (Psalm 118: 24) Let us learn, in other words, what it means to be truly glad. For the day of the Lord is manifestly different than other days. And the kind of gladness and rejoicing it calls for is unlike conventional conceptions of rejoicing which center around that which we think makes us happy. The triumphal entry involves the renunciation of triumphalism. Among other things, this means that that in which we are called to rejoice and that which makes us truly happy are not the sorts of things we might typically associate with victory and triumph: things like power, fame, honour, self-satisfaction, comfort, and the like. Each of these names a way of celebrating and fastening our hopes to that with which we are already familiar—most notably our sense of ourselves. But the day of the Lord names an alternative way of life, a way of life that is open to receiving the stranger, to that which we name as irreconcilably different. It was after all because Jesus was so completely strange, so entirely other, that he was put to death on the cross. And to speak of his resurrection is to come to recognize a way of life whereby the other is not treated as a conundrum to be figured out, whether violently or non-violently, but another being to be acknowledged.

To enter Holy Week is to be introduced to and redefined by what we might call God's time. God's time is a time which cannot be reconciled with other ways of understanding and inhabiting time. The passage of time is often inhabited in an essentially defensive posture of self-justification. History is narrated as a way of declaring our self-importance, our ongoing relevance. This happens most clearly when we read all prior history as somehow leading up to us—the source of hope, the bearers of progress, the cutting edge. We hear this when we hear it said that we are standing at the edge of history. This is surely one of the most clichéd and empty sayings of all time. And yet it continues to be said time and time again, especially by politicians or others who claim positions of "leadership." It is perhaps especially and most disturbingly prevalent when we find ourselves in the midst of war, as we do today. But that is why it is all the more important to revisit it, to unsettle it, and to find new—or perhaps old—meaning in it. What does it mean to speak of history in this way? And who is the "we" that is so confidently placed at its edge? Most often, to say that we are standing at the edge of history is to embark on an exercise in self-legitimation. It is an attempt to save ourselves. And yet such an attempt cannot but be exposed by the mysterious mind of Christ as a dangerous exercise in self-deception. The "we" that is named in such a claim are those who see themselves as the bearers of power. To utter such an uncomplicated "we" is to identify with those who are called into question by the redefinition of lordship that is central to the Christian confession of the lordship of Christ.

And yet there is a sense in which we are standing at the edge of history. It is not that history has come to an end and reached its terminus at the point where we happen to find ourselves standing. Nor is this to suggest that on the other side of the edge there is something that is altogether beyond history, something that exists outside of time. The great Christian ethicist Reinhold Niebuhr famously located the cross outside of history. But to locate the cross outside of history in this way is to make Jesus irrelevant so that he does not interfere with what we think needs to be done on the grounds of some sort of pragmatic calculation. It allows us to claim that Jesus is not a "political" figure, paving the way for us to be more "realistic" about the necessity of war from time to time. This is yet another way of insulating us against the possibility of serious self-critique. It is a way of making ourselves invulnerable—even, perhaps especially, to ourselves. It is to refuse the possibility of putting ourselves in question. Rather, if there is a truth to the claim that we are standing at the edge of history, it is that history, as understood from the perspective of Holy Week, is radically redefined.

To live in a time which is defined by the life, death, and resurrection of Christ is to inhabit a time that is untimely when measured by other ways of understanding time. It is not primarily about progress, but involves the recognition that we have more often than not fallen short of the model we were called by Paul to imitate. It does not involve exclusions, the setting of boundaries, and the policing of territories. But neither is it simply inclusive. That is just another way of redrawing and policing boundaries. Rather, it calls us to be vulnerable with one another, to love even our enemies. This is not an exercise in self-legitimation, a way of securing power, but an ongoing practice of dispossession, the work of renouncing possessive forms of power. Among other things, this should help us to recognize that history is not necessarily to be associated with the triumph of the good guys, or at least those whose "goodness" consists in the fact that we count them to be on "our side." Most importantly, God's time is not moved by violence. Rather, it is moved by God through those whose lives may be said to participate in the model of Christ identified by Paul—servants, the humble, those who empty themselves, those for whom others count more than themselves, those whose lives are lived as gifts to be given not as possessions to be controlled.

As central as these disruptive emphases may be, it is important to acknowledge that this is a difficult message to hear. It is not that we fail to hear them altogether. The point is too obvious to be entirely overlooked. But it is nevertheless difficult to hear it well. There is a tension between recognizing the call to have ourselves put in question and the task of receiving the full message of the words we claim to hear. I want to suggest that it is an attempt to point to this very struggle that is the main purpose of the texts we have been given to read this morning. For a recognition of the difficulty involved in receiving the message well is built into the passages themselves. Let us return to the psalmist once again. Having been told that the wisdom of God is built upon that stone that others have rejected, that God's wisdom flows against the stream of common sense, we read the following words: "Save us, we beseech you, O Lord! O Lord, we beseech you, give us success." (Psalm 118: 25) As I read it, the juxtaposition of these two lines is entirely jarring. For the preoccupation with our success is the very thing God's wisdom is calling into question. It is from our deep longing for salvation that God promises to save us.

This jarring tension is, of course, even further intensified in the story of the triumphal entry. As Jesus is riding into Jerusalem on a lowly donkey, the people place their robes on the ground, exalting him, and thereby treating him like the very sort of king he refuses to be. We want so badly to be glorified ourselves that we fail to see the glory of the one who refused to be glorified. We want so badly to be victorious that we fail to see the triumph of the one who renounced triumphalism. Jesus is not the kind of king who arrives in a gold-plated carriage and walks out onto a red carpet. He is not protected and kept safe by an entourage of gun-toting security guards. Rather, he is proclaimed as king, as messiah, because he exposed the lie of such a conception of kingship. He was the kind of king who dared to tread on the rough ground of ordinary human existence. He was, after all, born in a stable. He does not come to be protected from the messiness of life. He does not sidestep ugliness. Rather, he comes to embrace it. As the late British theologian Herbert McCabe has noted, Jesus did not belong to a "nice clean world" of honest and respectable people. His are not the kind of people who work hard, who repay their debts on time, who preserve societal order. In other words, Jesus does not belong to the kind of people who fill up churches like this one. He does not belong to the North American middle class. Rather, McCabe notes that his genealogy places him squarely in a "family of murderers, cheats, cowards, adulterers, and liars."[2] In other words, he belonged to *us*, to those same people that make up the North American middle class. And yet he came to address that part of us we have become so adept at denying. He came to us in a way that refused to bypass the vulgar nature of our existence. He came to make our very ordinary lives holy, and to find in ordinariness a certain kind of holiness. He came, in other words, to transform and redeem the ordinary. That is the mystery of God's wisdom. And it is because he dared to come to us in this way, a way that was so thoroughly like us that it seemed utterly foreign, completely strange, and entirely other, that he met the kind of end he did. That, we might say with Paul, is the scandal of the cross.

Part of the difficulty involved in being able to hear well the unsettling message of these passages is that we have a tendency to make them sound all too familiar. We have learned to read them in a way that removes or at least neuters the mystery to which they point. We have become masters at domesticating the disturbing messages of the Bible. Rowan Williams puts it this way:

> We brush aside the rumor of the cross and stick with the God we can do business with. This God is pleased with our bustle, our willingness to make him an absorbing, even an expensive, hobby. He is pleased that we treat our worship as something isolated and special, pleased by our religious professionalism. He is delighted that we so successfully manage the conditions under which he may be

---

[2] McCabe, *God Matters*, 249.

approached, saying "yes" to this one and "no" to that one, and "possibly, if you do the following things" to another.[3]

In other words, we almost habitually renarrate the biblical story in ways that we are able safely to manage. And in so doing, we fail to see that the heart of the message is that we are called to a way of life that passes beyond management. We are called out of the safe-making schemes we invent in order to save ourselves, to make ourselves feel safe. And we are called into a life of gift-giving and receiving, a way of life whereby we are made vulnerable to one another.

In case it isn't yet clear, all of this is but a way of exploring the topic of sin, on which I have been asked to speak this morning. More than anything else, sin names a refusal to allow ourselves to be put in question. It names our habit of domesticating God, of refusing to acknowledge the otherness of God. Sin names a way of life in which there is no space for the mystery of God's wisdom. It is a way of twisting the wisdom of God in such a way that it is rendered straightforward and unmysterious. It names a preoccupation with management and control. Put differently, sin is a conceit that arises from the temptation to think that we might be able to save ourselves. And more often than not, it is rooted in what we would identify as good intentions. We are often misled in our thinking about sin by a tendency to focus on what we might call the big sins, on those which are easy to identify. But perhaps even more important than avoiding the big sins is the ability to recognize the ordinariness of sin, what Hannah Arendt called the banality of evil. In trying to understand the nature of sin, we are better off looking at those everyday sins that arise from what we would identify as our good intentions. Augustine, in one of the classic Christian accounts of sin, claimed that sin is to be understood as something that is parasitic on the good. Sin is typically grounded in an attempt to do what we think of as good. Evil, for Augustine, does not name a positive reality. Metaphysically speaking, only good exists and evil is the privation of good. One implication of this is that sin has its roots in the very thing which might be said to overcome it. It is, in other words, rooted in Christ. In this respect, sin can be found in the way we make appeals to Christ as we strive to manage the world and as we set up boundaries in order to identify who belongs and who does not. Sin has its roots in the

---

[3] Williams, *A Ray of Darkness*, 46.

way we are able to turn the unsettling messages of the Bible into comforting messages of self-consolation.

The church is supposed to be a place where sin can be discussed. It is supposed to be a place where we can be honest with one another, where we can be vulnerable to one another, and in so doing become open to the possibility of forgiveness. But the great weakness of the church is that it often fails to be such a place. On the contrary, it tends to be a place where we come seeking confirmation. It is a place where we come to justify and legitimate ourselves rather than letting ourselves be put in question. Flannery O'Connor once spoke of the South as a place that was not so much Christ-centred as Christ-haunted. In doing so, she pointed to what both Augustine and the Bible identify as the central tension captured by the language of sin. I think she also instructively captured what it might mean for the church to be the church. As Paul reminds us, the church is to be a place where we learn to model our lives on Christ. In this respect, it is a place that is Christ-centred. And yet it is a place which does not rest easy in Christ. It is not merely centred in Christ but is also haunted by Christ. Indeed, it might be suggested that the root of sin consists in our tendency to separate the possibility of being Christ-centred from the necessity of being Christ-haunted.

How appropriate that these words are being delivered in a church called Hope. With all the emphasis on unsettling, on disruption, on haunting, and the form of temptation we call sin, it might seem as if I have set out to demolish our hope. But nothing could be further from the truth. These texts and the celebration of Palm Sunday that they frame are profoundly hopeful. Even as it passes through the darkness of the cross, Holy Week is the most hopeful of times. That is in part because it redefines hope. Our hope is that we have been given a hope that rests in something other than ourselves. Our hope involves the possibility of putting ourselves in question. Our hope makes possible a form of life that is triumphant precisely because it renounces triumphalism. It is in losing our hope that we may find it. This is the day that the Lord has made; let us rejoice and be glad in it.

Chapter 11

Suffering the Truth

Originally preached at Charleswood Mennonite Church, Winnipeg, MB
May 1, 2005, Sixth Sunday of Easter
Scripture Texts: Psalm 66: 8-20; 1 Peter 3:13-22; John 14: 15-21; Acts
17: 22-31

Cain murdered Abel, and blood cried out from the earth; the house fell on Job's children, and a voice was induced or provoked into speaking from a whirlwind; and Rachel mourned for her children; and King David for Absalom. The force behind the movement of time is a mourning that will not be comforted. That is why the first event is known to have been an expulsion, and the last is hoped to be a reconciliation and return. So memory pulls us forward, so prophecy is only brilliant memory—there will be a garden where all of us as one child will sleep with our mother Eve, hooped in her ribs and staved by her spine. ...

Memory is the sense of loss, and loss pulls us after it. God Himself was pulled after us into the vortex we made when we fell, or so the story goes. And while He was on earth He mended families. He gave Lazarus back to his mother, and to the centurion he gave a daughter again. He even restored the severed ear of the soldier who came to arrest him—a fact that allows us to hope the resurrection will reflect a considerable attention to detail. Yet this was no more than tinkering. Being a man He felt the pull of death, and being God He must have wondered more than we do what it would be like. He is known to have walked upon water, but he was not born to drown. And when he did die it was sad—such a young man, so full of promise, and His mother wept and His friends could not believe their loss, and the story spread everywhere and the mourning would not be comforted, until He was so sharply lacked and so powerfully remembered that his friends felt Him beside them as they walked along the road, and saw someone cooking fish on the shore and knew it to be Him, and sat down to supper with Him, all wounded as He was. There is so little to remember of anyone—an anecdote, a conversation at table. But every memory is turned over and over again, every word, however chance, written in the heart in the hope that the memory will fulfill itself, and become flesh, and that the wanderers will find a way home and the perished, whose lack we always feel, will step through the door finally and stroke our hair with dreaming, habitual fondness, not having meant to keep us waiting long.

—Marilynne Robinson, *Housekeeping*[1]

I open with these words from Marilynne Robinson's sparing yet powerfully evocative novel, *Housekeeping*, not only because they are among the most hauntingly beautiful words I have ever read—though they are that. Rather, I begin with this tragic but ultimately comedic and hopeful vision of memory and loss because it captures something that I take to be at the heart of the scripture passages we have been given this morning. *Housekeeping* is a story of two sisters, Ruth and Lucille. After the death of their grandfather in a catastrophic train wreck, and the suicide of their mother, who drove her car into the same glacial lake into which their grandfather plunged to his chilling demise, Ruth and Lucille finally settle with their Aunt Sylvie. And yet theirs is hardly a settled form of existence. It is a life of uncertain transience—of restless, almost nomadic wandering. Their lives can be said to inhabit an ongoing tension between memory and hope, between terrifying and traumatic loss and a promise of healing and reconciliation not yet fully experienced. In the end, Lucille opts for the lure of an apparently secure life of stable domesticity. Ruth, on the other hand, is left to struggle with the penetrating implications of homelessness and sorrow. It is from the mouth of Ruth that the words quoted above flow. Through the voice of Ruth, Robinson seeks to evoke an appreciation of dislocation and unsettlement that is at the very heart of faith. And yet hers is a homelessness that somehow strangely pulls her, almost in spite of herself, toward a more meaningful sense of home.

This is no idealistic utopianism. It is no cheap and easy faith. It is a profoundly theological vision of the very real but wounded truth of Christ. The story of Ruth can hardly be said to romanticize suffering.

---

[1] Robinson, *Housekeeping*, 192, 194-195.

Nor does it seek to give suffering some sort of intrinsic instrumental value. That would be perverse. Rather, Ruth's life suggests that any version of Christianity that offers a means to escape suffering cannot be the truth of Christ. For Robinson's characters, faith does not make life easier. It does, however, make their lives more worthwhile.[2] Her work can be seen as a powerful attempt to resist the temptation to read faith as a kind of belief in oneself, despite—or rather precisely because of—the insipid prevalence of this assumption in the contemporary American heartland in which she locates her writing. As one reviewer puts it, commenting on Robinson's disdain for what she identifies as the self-centred character of modern culture: "if Robinson rejects modernity, it is because modernity is so pleased with itself, and being pleased with yourself, in Robinson's world, is a dangerous way to be."[3] For Marilynne Robinson, faith is a dialectical virtue. It grows out of a sense of contradiction, of being at odds with oneself. It names a diasporic and unsettling experience of estrangement from that which we might otherwise consider home.

Memory and hope, loss and revelation, mourning and joy, expulsion and reconciliation, transience and home, death and resurrection, and, I might add finally, suffering and truth. Such is the strange and seemingly contradictory grammar of the Christian faith. Elsewhere, Robinson has suggested that "sermons are, at their best, excursions into difficulty."[4] It is the difficult, if not completely counter-intuitive, notion of suffering the truth that I have set out to explore this morning. To locate this question more clearly, let me turn to the collection of scripture passages we have before us. For there is a sense in which the tensions Ruth struggles with are reflected in the odd relationship that exists among these various texts. When read together, they conjure up a sense of mind-numbing paradox reminiscent of Søren Kierkegaard. On the one hand, the Psalm rings out with exuberant, almost triumphant praise to God, "who has kept us among the living." The Psalm might be read as a hymn of thanksgiving to God who has and will take care of us, who

---

[2] Ian Chang, "Mapping the Lost Heartland: A Review of Marilynne Robinson's Gilead," *The Philadelphia Independent*, February, 2005.

[3] Ibid.

[4] Marilynne Robinson, "Interview: Marilynne Robinson," *Religion & Ethics Newsweekly* (website), posted March 18, 2005. https://www.pbs.org/wnet/religionandethics/2005/03/18/march-18-2005-interview-marilynne-robinson/4226/

promises to put an end to our suffering. God will thus bring us safely home, or at least "to a spacious place" in which we are secure from the threats of fire and water or from people riding over our heads. On the other hand, as if to counter the unwarranted optimism that might result from a shallow reading of such a passage, Peter highlights the very real prospect of suffering and loss. He offers a counter-intuitive sort of encouragement to his listeners, telling them "it is better to suffer for doing good, if suffering should be God's will." Moreover, he warns that suffering is not merely a theoretical possibility, but that it is entirely likely that some will "suffer for doing what is right." He counters, however, with the consolation that those who do so will be blessed.

What is going on here? First we seem to be presented with a hopeful vision of a victorious God who promises to overcome suffering, to bring reconciliation, and so to return us safely home. And then, as if to have our hope cruelly snatched away from us, we are faced with the cold reality of suffering and sorrow. We are told that even Christ suffered, and that those who follow him will be abused for their "good conduct in Christ." Or at least that is how things look if we merely skim the surface of these passages. But I wonder if these texts have been placed together in the lectionary precisely because of the strong temptation to push each of them to extremes if we read them in isolation. I want to suggest that these two passages serve to highlight a difficulty—namely that faithfulness is not a guarantee of security and success—and that the additional passage from John is an attempt to deepen our understanding of this difficulty. We should then read John as an attempt to offer some sort of clarification of the tension that exists between hopeful memory and sorrowful loss. The problem, however, is that John's account works just to the extent that it fails to make things any easier. The key text here would be Jesus' words, "This is the spirit of truth, whom the world cannot receive, because it neither sees him nor knows him." (John 14:17) The Gospel of John is built around the conviction that Christ is indeed the truth. And this is reason for praise and hope. The only problem is that the world does not—indeed John says *cannot*—recognize this. And so those who set out to proclaim the truth of Christ are left in a rather precarious position of having something to say that will not be heard. John can thus be read as an attempt to reckon with the implications of the Christian insistence on speaking of Christ as the incarnate truth. In doing so, he pushes our standard and all-too-comfortable notions of truth to the most extreme limits. Recall that later on in John we hear

Pilate, at his wits end, dismissively cry out "what is truth?" Pilate recognizes that the truth Christ would embody puts much of what we otherwise want to claim as truth radically into question. I suspect it is out of an appreciation of this sort of difficulty about the truth of Christ that Ruth's sense of dislocation arises. The truth of Christ is not that of the world. And yet we who claim to be shaped by it also live in the world. And so Christianity names a life that is simultaneously truthful wisdom and the most absurd folly.

Like Pilate, we are unaccustomed to thinking of truth as something suffered. We tend to think of it, rather, as something discovered. Our customary ways of speaking about truth imply that it is somehow inert and just sits there, awaiting our potential recognition of it. We typically understand truth by invoking images of a knowing subject who grasps, captures, or takes hold of an object waiting to be known. In so doing, we assume that truth is static and is entirely dependent on our activity if it is to have any power. And yet reading John against the background of the passages from Psalms and 1 Peter suggests that truth is better described as something suffered. It does not turn upon something we do, but rather is something that happens to us. Here we seem to be presented with a view of truth that is exactly the opposite of that which we normally assume. It is not that we are active in discovering a truth that resides somehow beyond us in an independent realm of objectivity. Rather, the truth of Christ is active and comes to us. Notice that John speaks of truth as something *received*. It is the work of the spirit. In such an understanding of truth, our activity or agency is relativized in a way. Among other things, I take it that John is offering a contrarian vision of truth that serves to save us from our tendency to deceive ourselves by aspiring to a truth we might possibly reach by using our own resources.

With Rowan Williams, let us understand the knowledge of God not as "a subject's conceptual grasp of an object," but rather as "sharing what God is."[5] Knowledge of God, so construed, involves conformity with God—a conformity that can only happen by God first coming to us. So reflecting on the theme of truth in the Gospel of John, Williams writes:

Living in truth means living where Jesus lives. In the farewell discourses [from which our passage this morning is taken], the shadow of the passion of Jesus constantly shows the horizon, and it

---

[5] Williams, *The Wound of Knowledge*, 13.

is obviously part of being where Jesus is that the believer shares in Jesus' vulnerability and death. Jesus' friends will be hated as he is hated. When Jesus speaks of being 'consecrated in the truth,' the reader is immediately invited to connect this with Jesus; 'consecration' of himself, which can only mean the death he is to endure. Truth and death are brought together with alarming closeness: truthful living is the full acceptance of the real and concrete danger of pursuing faithfulness in this world: it is an acceptance of risk and mortality.[6]

Williams suggests, further, that the entire Gospel of John is to be read as a kind of "challenge to the 'insider'."[7] He claims that "John's theme is that those who consciously identify themselves as the ones who really believe or really know are also those who cannot bear the light that comes from Christ."[8] And so we return to Ruth's unsettled struggles with dislocation, memory and loss. Robinson's theological vision of expulsion and reconciliation is located in the person of Ruth because she has come closest to living as an outsider in the way Jesus did. But Ruth's life is finally hopeful because she embodies truth as something suffered. In doing so, she helps us appreciate what I have elsewhere called the "agony of truth."[9] Such a truth can be considered absolute only in its experience of vulnerable fragility. How odd to think of the truth as something suffered. And yet, come to think of it, how strangely wonderful. Such a vision of truth cannot but be an unwelcome interruption in a world obsessed with possession, security, and control. But Ruth, like Jesus, performs just such an interruption. And in so doing, she offers us a glimpse of a world in which we might be freed from the tyranny of placing our hope in our own powers. Perhaps this is what John means when elsewhere he has Jesus say, "you will know the truth, and the truth will make you free." Thanks be to God.

---

[6] Williams, *Christ on Trial*, 78.

[7] Ibid., 74.

[8] Ibid., 74.

[9] Huebner, *A Precarious Peace*, 133-144.

Chapter 12

Ascension, Atheism,
and the Strange Body of Christ

Originally preached at Charleswood Mennonite Church
May 6, 2010, Ascension Sunday
Scripture Texts: Acts 1:1-11; Ephesians 1:15-23; Luke 24:44-53

Sometime during the first few weeks of the semester, I typically inform the students in my "Introduction to Christianity" class that the early Christians were regarded with suspicion by their Roman neighbours because the Romans considered them to be atheists. By this point in the semester, we have already examined how we might make sense of Jesus telling his followers that they should hate their mothers and fathers. (Luke 14:26) At the very least, this suggests that Christianity cannot be regarded as any sort of straightforward family values movement. Nor can it be about love in any ordinary sense of the term. We have also noted that these same early Christians horrified their neighbors by engaging in practices that pagan Romans understood to represent a sort of death cult. They gathered for worship on and around the tombs of the dead. And in addition to regularly touching and kissing the bodies of the dead, they frequently dug them up and brought them along on their journeys. When compared with early Christian worship practices, it was the pagan Romans who are best described as "pro-life."

As you might guess, these sorts of observations do not always go over terribly well at first blush. There may even be an occasional student or two who runs straight for the academic advisor's office to pick up a course withdrawal form. And yet as strange as all this might sound to contemporary ears, these are some of the clearest ways in which early Christians came to be differentiated from other forms of religious life. So before you resolve never to let your children attend CMU, let me assure you that I do go on to spend the rest of the semester trying to help students make sense of these claims and how they might be understood in relation to the subsequent history of Christianity. This is not just an attempt to mess with the minds of naïve 18 year olds for the fun of it. Rather, this rather shocking and somewhat offensive collection of observations serves an important pedagogical function. It prepares students for the realization that Christianity is an entirely strange sort of phenomenon. Moreover, it gives them a sense that Christianity is distorted when it is dressed up in pieties that serve to domesticate it. It helps them see that Christianity is somehow at odds with itself when it becomes something familiar and comfortable. So while these biblical and historical expressions of the strangeness of Christianity run the risk of losing some, I think it is a risk well worth taking. Indeed, I think this is a risk we must take if we are to be faithful to the event we are celebrating this morning, namely the ascension of Christ.

But first, let us return to the question of why the early Christians were described as atheists. Pagan Romans were accustomed to dealing with gods who were in some sense present and near at hand. They worshipped gods which were thought to be closely bound up and involved with the social order in which ordinary Roman life was situated. Indeed, the gods were seen as guarantors of their social and political order. One became a good citizen of that society by interacting with the gods in a whole variety of direct and tangible ways. The gods might be described as representatives of the status quo. In some ways, it might help to think of them as levers by which to exert some form of power. In order to get things done, you needed to appeal to the gods. That is why there were so many of them. There are many things that need to happen in order to make a society work. And so we find a whole range of gods, each of which is charged with the task of governing a particular sphere of life. There is a sense in which it might be described as mechanistic and technological. At the same time, given the under-riding desire to preserve the order of world, we might say that paganism is an inherently conservative religion.

Christianity was viewed as an affront to this entire way of thinking. Not only do Christians worship one God. Theirs is a God who is absent from the usual mechanisms of power and control that define the world. By "absence" here, I mean to suggest that God does not play that same sort of game. God is simply not involved in the maintenance and preservation of a social order. Relative to the game of what we might call power politics, the Christian God is nowhere to be found. The God of Jesus Christ cannot therefore be appealed to as a lever that functions to create and sustain a society. When it comes to the status quo, our God is absent, a non-participant. Indeed, the Christian God represents a profound critique of social and political order. Or at least that is how the Romans saw it. Another way to put this is to say that obedience to the Jewish and Christian God trumps obedience to the emperor. That is why there were so many early Christian martyrs. The martyrs were those who went to their deaths because they refused to pledge allegiance to the emperors or to the gods of pagan Rome. All of this is a reflection of the fact that Christianity is not first of all about managing and maintaining order. It is not about security and control. And it is not about preserving power as we usually think about it. Rather, as the apostle Paul puts it, it is about faith, hope, and love.

To put it this way suggests a very different way of approaching the debates about atheism that are said to be flourishing at the moment. We have become accustomed to thinking of atheism as an enemy that threatens the established role of religion. Indeed, it is often suggested that atheism must be resisted because it threatens the very foundation of our social order. It is a small step from atheism, many religious commentators suggest, to nihilistic despair and destruction. What I find most interesting here is the apparent ease with which Christians assume a position of being on the defensive. They speak as if from a position of power that suddenly finds itself under siege. How far we have come. Early Christians were defined as atheists because theirs was a God who was absent from the established social order. Contemporary Christians find themselves inclined to attack atheism because of the way it threatens the role of religion as a pillar of our social order. I hope it goes without saying that there is a big difference between the so-called atheism of the early Christians and the contemporary atheism of a Richard Dawkins or a Christopher Hitchens. But it is just as important to recognize that there is a world of difference between the faith of the early Christian martyrs and the faith of those contemporary Christians who set out to defend an intellectual position called "theism." I think that these two differences are at least in part bound up with the doctrine of Christ's ascension.

The ascension accounts are some of the clearest ways in which the Bible speaks about the absence of the Christian God in the sense that it came to be associated with the early Christians. To present Jesus as ascending into heaven is to say that he is absent or somehow set apart from the world as we know it. It is a way of portraying God as one who is not in sync with the sorts of assumptions and structures we usually take for granted. This is why the Bible portrays Jesus as travelling upwards. It is a way of demonstrating that Christ rules over the powers. This is also why Paul's account of the ascension depicts Christ as sitting at the right hand of God the Father. (Eph 1:20) This is the position from which judgement is enacted. We still speak this way today. For example, we refer to someone whose task it is to help execute a leader's authority as a "right hand man." The ascension is thus the biblical way of saying that Christ stands as a judge over against the world. To put it somewhat paradoxically, he judges and in so doing transforms the forms of judgement to which we customarily find ourselves drawn.

Notice that in the book of Acts, Jesus rebukes his followers for asking whether this is the time for the kingdom of Israel to be restored. He castigates them for once again taking him to be the sort of king who rules by way of calculative political power. He tells them, "it is not for you to know the times or the seasons which the Father has fixed by his own authority." (Acts 1:7) He seems to be saying, here, that they should not be looking for mechanisms by which they can move history in the right direction. And then he makes reference to a different sort of power, the power of the Holy Spirit. He suggests that this is a kind of power that is given and received. It is not the sort of power that is wielded as if it were a possession of some kind. It is not sitting "out there" somewhere, suggesting that we might find it if only we could accumulate enough knowledge and information. Rather, he simply says it will "come upon you." This gives the impression that it is not something earned. Nor is it something we are owed. Rather, he suggests that we will receive it in spite of ourselves. And it was at this point that "he was lifted up, and a cloud took him out of their sight." (Acts 1:9) All of these themes are echoed in Paul, who writes to the Ephesians that Christ is "far above all rule and authority and power and dominion." (Eph 1:21) By situating the ascension in the context of these claims, we can hear it as a way of questioning the establishment of certain alleged givens.

And yet it is all too easy to think of ascension precisely as a kind of establishment or confirmation. And similarly with the resurrection. We tend to think of the resurrection along the lines of a sort of proof. The resurrection is thought to establish the fact that Jesus is who his followers have thought him to be. It is read as confirming the memory of Jesus once and for all. In this regard, it is taken to function as a sort of divine "I told you so." It is a way of saying to one's detractors, "see, we were right all along!" And then ascension is understood to drive this point home even more forcefully. Not only is Jesus resurrected from the dead. He is then raised even higher, such that he is seated at the right hand of the father. In this way, the ascension is related to the resurrection as a way of upping the ante of our confidence even further. It functions as a rhetorical exclamation point, perhaps the primary exclamation point of the New Testament. In some respects, all of this is true. For without the resurrection and ascension of Christ, Jesus would be just another guy with a habit of saying and doing things that got him into trouble. But at the same time, this truth should not obscure the profoundly subversive edge that runs through the Christian belief in the ascension of Christ. I have been trying to suggest that the ascension functions at least as much as a question mark as an exclamation point. It is a question mark that is placed on our temptation to treat Christ as a lever by which to establish a social order in the manner of the Roman appeal to their gods.

And yet this should not obscure the fact that the ascension does establish a kind of social order. In both of the passages we have heard this morning, it is very clearly linked to the founding of the church. When I said earlier that the Christian God is absent from the world governed by the Roman gods, it is not that God is altogether or absolutely absent, as if to suggest a sort of mysterious vapor that hovers transcendently above the material world. Recall that the early Christians were a people of the body. This is why they had such profound relationships with the dead. Take away the body and take away the bodies of the dead and you've essentially taken away Christianity. The church is, after all, described as the body of Christ. But at the same time, the body of Christ is not a body like other bodies. In particular, it is not simply or straightforwardly "there." It does not function as a site of power over which we might think of ourselves as being in control.

This is what Paul is trying to get at with his rather confusing talk of flesh and spirit, talk that is very closely related to the theme of ascension. It is crucial to understand that spirit for Paul does not name a different kind of reality that is to be distinguished from the material reality of the body. Paul did not conceive of human beings as made up of two different kinds of stuff, a material fleshy stuff and an immaterial spiritual stuff. Rather, spirit is his way of talking about how the body is ordered or organized. In short, it is a body that is ordered to a loving God who comes to us as a gift rather than a body that is pridefully turned in upon on itself. So what sounds to modern ears like a metaphysical dualism between body and soul is really, for Paul, a portrayal of two very different kinds of bodies. One he calls flesh or world or the powers. The other he calls spirit or church, the very body of Christ. The logic of spirit and ascension can thus be seen as a different way of thinking about being, power, love, etc. This is why Jesus tells us to hate our fathers and mothers. In the political context of his day, it was through the family that power was secured. By contrast, the body of Christ is a social body whose life is lived out of control.

In theological jargon, the ascension is often associated with what we call a high Christology. It is also assumed to be something that we Mennonites are uncomfortable with. Mennonites are usually assumed to be more interested in the Jesus of the Gospels. We like to think of ourselves as a practical people. And so we are interested in the life of Jesus, his example and his parables, the biblical material in which the stuff of ethics and politics can be found. We are thought to be less interested in the heady, metaphysical speculation required to make sense of resurrection and ascension. But I think this is a mistake, albeit a mistake to which Mennonites sometimes find themselves drawn. If my depiction of ascension is correct, it is just as much "low" as it is "high." That is to say, it is not a flight from the "practical" stuff of ethics or politics. On the contrary, it is very closely bound up with an understanding of the social that questions our investment in mechanisms of security and control. It challenges the sorts of impulses that lead us to turn so quickly to violence when things do not play out as we'd like. To celebrate the ascension of Christ is to acknowledge that Jesus inaugurates a very different way of being and acting, a peaceable kingdom. In the words of Paul, "God put this power to work in Christ when he raised him from the dead and seated him at his right hand up in the heavenly places, far above all rule and authority and power and dominion, and above every name that is named, not only in this age but also in the age to come." (Eph. 1: 20-21)

Chapter 13

Let Your Love Overflow with Knowledge

Originally preached at CMU Baccalaureate Service
April 24, 2016, Graduation Sunday
Scripture Reading: Philippians 1: 3-11

Let me start with a story. You might even call it a love story. But really it's an unusual story about a girl named Love. Although she was just a young child, Love was known for her dazzling beauty, for her dedication to the Christian faith, and for being precociously wise beyond her years. It was especially because of the last of these qualities that she found herself in the company of the Roman Emperor Hadrian in the early part of the second century. Hadrian also had a reputation as someone who possessed remarkable intellectual capacities. And so he summoned for Love to appear before him. Hadrian showered Love with praise for both her beauty and her intelligence. But he was less than impressed with her commitment to the Christian faith. He offered to take Love in as his own daughter and promised that he would dedicate himself to the task of helping her realize her extraordinary intellectual potential. But he insisted on one crucial condition, that she renounce her belief in Christ. Not only did Love refuse his offer. She is said to have mocked the Emperor's knowledge and called him a fool before serenading him with hymns of praise to her lord Jesus Christ.

Needless to say, the Emperor Hadrian was unaccustomed to this sort of defiant response and he did not take to it very kindly. His generosity immediately turned to violent rage and he subjected Love to a series of the most savage tortures. First, she was placed on a rack and stretched, her limbs tearing out of their sockets one by one. At this point, Hadrian offered Love a final opportunity to renounce her faith and offer a sacrifice to goddess Artemis. Once again, she refused. So he ordered his guards to throw her into a white-hot furnace. Love is said to have walked into the furnace on her own volition. But surprisingly, she was unharmed by the intense fire. Antiochus, Hadrian's right-hand man, reported that Love playfully "walked among the flame-spewing vapours, quite unhurt, and sang hymns of praise to her God."[1] She eventually walked out of the furnace, entirely unharmed. The furnace, on the other hand, did not fare so well. It exploded, killing some of the bystanders and even singeing the Emperor himself. The Emperor then had her seized for a third time and ordered that she be beheaded by the sword. This third punishment proved to be too much to bear and so Love succumbed to death by decapitation. In doing so, she died in the same manner as her older sisters, Faith and Hope, who perished before her. Their mother, whose name was Wisdom and who witnessed all three of their deaths, took the dead bodies of her daughters and buried them outside the Roman city. After praying at their grave for three days, she herself died. All four of them were awarded the purple crown of martyrdom. Their martyrdom is still recognized by many Christian churches today. In the Eastern Orthodox Church, their feast is celebrated on September 17. In the Roman Catholic tradition, it is celebrated on August 1.

Now, some of you are probably wondering about the appropriateness of such a story given the context of our gathering today. Scenes of torture and death at a graduation service? Way to wreck a good mood. Let me assure you that this is not an attempt to correct for the excessive happiness and sense of accomplishment many of you might be feeling today. Neither does it reflect a fascination, let alone a glorification, of suffering and death as if these things are somehow good in and of themselves. The reason there are so many stories about dying in early Christianity is because the unit of moral and spiritual evaluation was understood to be an entire life. To put it very simply, Christianity was in some ways less concerned with particular beliefs and actions than it was with the overall shape of one's life. As the historian John Bossy puts it, Christianity was less a body of beliefs than it was a body of believers.[2] Because what matters for such a discussion is the story of a complete life, the question of how one dies is very much a part of the equation. Martyrs are those whose deaths are consistent with lives that are lived in friendship with Christ. In other words, it is not merely *that* one dies but *how* one dies—the manner of one's death—that makes someone a martyr.

---

[1] Hrotsvit, "The Martyrdom of the Holy Virgins Fides, Spes, and Karitas," 145.

[2] Bossy, *Christianity in the West: 1400-1700*, 167-171.

Let me give you just one example. In early Christian martyr stories, Christians are frequently depicted as somehow managing to survive fire, just as Love did. Why might this be? For at least two important reasons. First, there is the story of the fiery furnace in the book of Daniel. And second, fire was understood as a symbol of forgetting. So to tell a story of someone in which they are said not to perish in a fire is to say that this is a person who did not forget their faith in Christ. It is important to understand that early Christians did not understand faith to name a collection of beliefs. In early Christianity, faith was a habit, a virtue, that structured lives around the acknowledgement that life is gift. Accordingly, it follows that to speak of "not forgetting" faith is not simply to stress the capacity for cognitive recall, where one is said to hold fast to a set of theoretical convictions. Rather, it is more like remembering who—or whose—you are. In other words, those who survive fire are those whose lives are understood somehow to be permeated by the biblical story. They are friends of Christ and other biblical figures like Shadrach, Meshach, and Abednego. And all of this is quite independent of the empirical question of how anyone might have actually died. Tales of early Christian martyrs are not to be read as if they were newspaper reports. The rejection of fire as the cause of someone's death is not a claim that could be contradicted by an autopsy report. So how, then, do Christians die? They typically die in one of two ways: by crucifixion or beheading. And why is that? Once again, the short answer is Jesus and John the Baptist. The longer answer, at least with respect to death by beheading, has something to do with the question of knowledge. Which is what takes us back to the story of Love and how it relates to the graduation verse you have drawn from Paul's letter to the Philippians.

If you are with me this far, you will appreciate that the story about Love has little to do with the question of objective facts as we might understand them. So to ask whether or not these events really took place, as many of us are inclined to do, is really to miss the point of the story. Neither is it to be read subjectively, as a story that invites us to reflect on Love's experiences and feelings. Rather, the story of Love is an allegory. Allegories are stories in which concepts are personified. Characters and events are deployed as a way of interpreting ideas and their meanings. The story of Love is an allegory that sets out to display conceptual connections. More specifically, I want to suggest that it draws attention to a series of conceptual connections that run throughout many of Paul's letters. How so?

Recall that Love is one of three daughters of Wisdom. Her two sisters were named Faith and Hope. Collectively, then, Wisdom and her daughters can be seen to represent a way of knowing that is in conformity with Christ and is at odds with that of the world, here represented by the Emperor Hadrian. In fact, Hadrian's reputation as a person of knowledge is significant precisely in that it is presented as representative of a kind of pseudo-knowledge. Hadrian does not embody knowledge, Love insists, but foolishness. Does that sound familiar? Paul regularly draws distinctions between different kinds of knowledge. These distinctions are most clearly and forcefully stated in his first letter to the church in Corinth. The Corinthians, he thinks, are confused about knowledge. And so Paul tries to clarify things for them by dismissing some forms of knowledge and affirming others. Sometimes he puts this in terms of a contrast between wisdom and knowledge. Knowledge, he says, "will come to an end." (1 Cor. 13:8) When it does, it will give way to wisdom. At other times, Paul speaks of a contrast between two kinds of wisdom: the wisdom of the cross and the wisdom of the world. (1 Cor. 18-25) Each of these will be regarded as foolishness from the standpoint of the other. Elsewhere, his manner of speech is more paradoxical, suggesting that it is knowledge itself that is somehow the enemy of knowledge, as when he says "anyone who claims to know something does not yet have the necessary knowledge." (1 Cor. 8:2) Similar themes are echoed in his letter to the Romans. Here, for example, he informs his audience that they must be transformed by having their minds renewed. (Rom. 12:2) There is knowledge and then there is knowledge, Paul seems to be saying. "Great, thanks Paul," I can feel most of you saying to yourselves. "That really clears things up. Care to elaborate?"

Reading Paul can be a disorienting affair. He leaves us with our heads spinning, asking questions like "Whose knowledge? Which wisdom?" How are we supposed to understand all these distinctions and qualifications he keeps throwing at us? This is where love comes in. For it is the theological virtues of faith, hope, and love—but especially love—that Paul points to as the difference makers when it comes to knowledge. This is especially clear in 1 Corinthians 13, in a passage that has for some strange reason come to be associated with weddings: "If I speak in the tongues of mortals and angels, but do not have love, I am a noisy gong and a clanging symbol. And if I have prophetic powers, and understand all mysteries and all knowledge, and if I have all faith, so as to remove mountains, but do not have love, I am nothing." (1 Cor. 13: 1-2) Knowledge, as we noted above, will come to an end. But Paul insists that "love never ends." (1 Cor. 13:8)

Paul's displacement of knowledge by love is the key to the conceptual connections that the story of Love and her sisters sets out to make. It identifies wisdom as a kind of knowledge that is informed by the theological virtues of faith, hope, and love. This way of knowing will look radically different than other ways of knowing that are not shaped by these virtues, such as that of Hadrian. But at the same time it is important to recognize that it is less about what we know than it is about how we know or what our knowing looks like. It is not so much a question of the content of our knowledge as it is a matter of form or style. It might help to think of all this in athletic terms, another theme that runs throughout many of Paul's letters, not to mention the logic of martyrdom. In the early church, for example, martyrs were known as "athletes of God." Paul speaks of knowledge as a capacity that needs to be cultivated, trained, and perfected. Knowledge, then, passes away and is transformed into wisdom when it is stripped of its bad habits and reconstituted around good habits of thought such as love.

So let us come back, finally, to take a closer look at the verse chosen by the class of 2016 to commemorate their graduation: "this is my prayer, that your love overflow more and more with knowledge and full insight." I suspect many of us hear this and almost instinctively place the emphasis on the words "knowledge and full insight." This might be especially tempting given that we are gathered here in the context of a university. Those of us who spend our lives in universities are especially prone to assuming that knowledge will solve all of our problems. To read the verse this way suggests that it is knowledge, cool and objective, that governs love, which is otherwise prone to being distorted by the heat of passion. Knowledge is necessary so that we might love the right things or people in the right sorts of ways. But I hope it is clear by now that this cannot be the correct way to understand the relationship between knowledge and love as Paul speaks of it. For Paul, it is love that disciplines and informs knowledge, not the other way around. To say that love overflows with knowledge is to speak of a way of knowing that is shaped by the sort of love that Christ exemplified.

So what difference might this make with respect to the question of knowledge? Notice how natural it is to think of knowledge as something grasped or held. We speak as if truth is a possession that we can somehow seize hold of. We describe potential knowledge as something that is within reach. We also speak of truth claims, suggesting that truth involves a kind of entitlement, a form of ownership. And we do this equally, some might say especially, when it comes to thinking about Christianity. But to do so is to be a lousy lover. Paul would have us envision knowledge not as a form of ownership and possession, as these habits of speech suggest, but as gift. Knowledge informed by love is performed as a sort of charitable exchange. This sort of knowledge is not ours to protect and secure but is something essentially shared. Moreover, it is as much something we receive from others as it is something we give. It arises from attentive listening as much as it does from powerful speaking. That we can so love in the first place is only because we have been first loved. By Christ, yes. But also by those strangers in whose faces we fail to recognize Christ. For let us never forget that Christ always appears as a stranger. And so a knowledge informed by love will be vulnerable and humble. It will also be wild and surprising. And here's another funny thing. If this is something that takes training and disciplined work, there is also a sense in which it is training in the art of letting go. It is an undisciplined mind that thinks of knowledge as a thing we must hold on to tightly. It takes disciplined striving to see it as a gift of love. That we will fail in this enterprise of having our minds renewed is not really in question. We will most certainly fail. But how we handle such failure is, as always, where the rubber hits the road. Among other things, one thing we should never assume is that we are somehow alone in all of this. A knowledge informed by love is joyous work that is performed in the company of good friends—friends who know us better than we know ourselves.

None of this will make any sense as long as we continue to think of love as an emotion and knowledge as a collection of facts. But if love is a way of being among others and knowledge is an informed practice or performance, then all sorts of new and interesting possibilities start to emerge. It is my hope you got at least a taste of some of these possibilities during the time you spent studying at CMU. So in closing, let me speak on behalf of the faculty of CMU, echoing the words of Paul in saying that this is our prayer for you, that your love overflow more and more with knowledge. But let me also express a heartfelt word of gratitude to all of you for being such great lovers. I suspect I am not alone in thinking that many of you have taught us as much about what love-informed knowledge looks like as anything we might have taught you. For the gift of your good love, and for your companionship in this strange adventure of seeking wisdom, we give thanks.

Chapter 14

I Feel Jesus in the Tenderness of Honest, Nervous Lovers:
A Tribute to the CMU Graduating Class of 2011

April 15, 2011, Graduation weekend

In his 2005 J. J. Thiessen Lectures, Paul Griffiths argued that we should not understand the work of the university as a diverse collection of experts, each of whom governs a discreet field of knowledge. Rather, he suggested that we see the intellectual life as an expression of the sort of dedication and commitment we attribute to the amateur. By "amateur" Griffiths did not just mean that we should give ourselves more freedom to range widely and wildly across various disciplines of the university as specialists in a kind of non-specialization. Rather, he meant that we should approach our work as an expression of love. Some of you will recognize, I hope, that the root for the word amateur is the Latin word *amare*—to love. So Griffiths gives us an image of the intellectual life as a love-soaked and profoundly erotic enterprise. It is about the pursuit of truth, yes. But the nature of that pursuit is not one of conquest and mastery so much as it is a form of desire in which truth is simply enjoyed for its own sake.[1]

This means that we should imagine the pursuit of truth in a way that is analogous to how we approach the pursuit of other things we claim to love. Among other things, this means that the appropriate language in which to speak of truth is that of beauty and attraction rather than usefulness. There is, of course, something deeply theological and philosophical about all this. I could turn to Augustine or Aquinas or Dante to develop this point. We could also look at Shakespeare or Stanley Cavell. And that's not even to mention any number of biblical

---

[1] For a fuller elaboration of this vision of the intellectual life, see Griffiths, *The Vice of Curiosity*.

examples. But instead, I will quote one of my favourite bands of the moment—the Hold Steady. I'm thinking in particular of their song "Citrus," which contains the following lines: "I feel Jesus in the clumsiness of young and awkward lovers. I feel Judas in the long odds of the rackets on the corners. I feel Jesus in the tenderness of honest, nervous lovers."

Without getting into all the juicy the details, let me just say that I think both Griffiths and the Hold Steady are, despite their very different contexts, saying something quite similar. And I hope CMU is the kind of place where we might at least get a few glimpses or tastes of this vision and how it might play out in the context of the university. Of course, the key implication of all this is that we are first of all lovers. And to put it that way runs the risk of wandering into territory that is distinctly awkward, if not entirely inappropriate. It is surely no accident that literature and film return time and again to the genre of erotic attraction between teachers and students. Because our work is fundamentally a work of love, it should not come as a surprise that the risk of these sorts of distortions always lurks dangerously close by. But that is not the kind of love I have in mind here. To see professors and students primarily as lovers of each other is to get the wrong sort of picture. Rather, the point is that we are, together, lovers of the truth. Our love is only secondarily directed at other objects or persons. It is first of all ordered to and by the truth we call God. We love each other, if at all, as participants in a shared love of truth whose beauty is endlessly enjoyable.

One of the greatest joys of teaching at a place like CMU is the opportunity to be intimately involved in a project that seeks to nourish growth in this ongoing pursuit of love. It is not uncommon for students to show up armed with an assortment of clumsy and awkward gestures of random adolescent groping. Most of you are here because you've got a crush on some slice of the truth. And this is frequently the result of having been inspired by some previous teacher. From there, we typically see an extended period of experiments that are perhaps best described as instances of serial monogamy. This is the period in which students are pushed to identify their loves in terms of the discourse of majors and minors. If you are anything like the statistically normal student, there will be a couple of switches in your academic program before you finally settle on your true love. Here we find students moving from one relationship to the next, each of them pursued with a passion that is equally serious. But all of them are doomed to fail if they are approached with an intensity that is too fierce and an exclusivity that is too narrow. Think of this as the academic expression of jealousy, which arises from approaching our loves in a manner that is inherently possessive. And yet if all goes well, we come to graduation, where students leave the university as the kind of tender, honest lovers about which the Hold Steady sing. It is appropriate for lovers of this sort to be nervous because we know how fragile such love is.

To witness the random groping of adolescent lust grow into more mature forms of love is, I suspect, something that is way more beautiful than anything any of us thought we'd experience when we got into this business we call the university. I hope each and every one of you is able to say that you leave CMU having fallen deeply in love with something you have encountered in this place. But more importantly, I hope you have acquired an ability to hold onto your loves loosely, as they deserve to be held. On behalf of the rest of the faculty at CMU, I want to say a sincere thank-you for sharing your intellectual love lives with us. I hope each of us has modeled in some way what such a love of truth might look like. We love you guys and wish you all the best as you leave us to encounter a new group of young and awkward lovers.

Chapter 15

The Joy of (Re)marriage:
A 50th Anniversary Tribute
to Agnes and Harry Huebner

Originally delivered at Bangkok Thai Restaurant, Winnipeg, MB
August 21, 2016

Mom is a Hildebrand. And being Hildebrand means being involved in programs. Every family gathering and even some informal get-togethers required a program of some sort. I used to hate this. Truth be told, I still find it difficult to get excited about the inevitable point when someone announces it is time for the program. But I've come to realize that my opinion about these matters doesn't really matter. This is just what we Hildebrands do and it is an important part of who we are. As much as Mom and Dad insisted in the last several months that they did not want a big program at their anniversary celebration, we all knew that some sort of program would be a necessary part of this event. And we also knew that most of the roles in this program would be assigned by Mom. My assignment, as I'm sure you've guessed by now, is to say a few words. She suggested I say something that was "philosophical and theological." "For Dad," she added. A speech delivered to an audience of one is more than a little awkward. So I hope there's something in here that resonates with Mom and the rest of you too.

I'm sure philosophy and theology are probably the last thing many of you might be hoping for at an anniversary celebration. What could a philosopher possibly have to say about marriage? Philosophers are supposed to be concerned with the possibility of knowledge, the question of other minds, and other sorts of epistemological and metaphysical problems. Moreover, the common image of a philosopher is typically not an image of someone who is accomplished in the arts of relationship. Our common impression of the philosopher is that he or she is socially awkward at best. At worst, they are entirely anti-social. Or at any rate, they have a remarkable capacity to alienate a crowd. Think, for example, of Socrates. The founding father of philosophy had a distinct knack for making everyone else uncomfortable. And the theologian hardly fares any better. While the sermon may be an important part of a wedding ceremony, let's be honest: how often don't we approach the wedding sermon as something you simply have to endure in order to make it to the really good part?

But if that's our knee-jerk reaction to the worlds of philosophy and theology, let me suggest that it is a profound mistake. To be sure, it is a mistake for which philosophers and theologians have nobody to blame but themselves. Nevertheless, I want to suggest that the question of marriage is actually at the heart of both philosophy and theology. If nothing else, I do not think it is an accident that the most interesting and important philosophers and theologians make it a central feature of their work. Let me illustrate this by reflecting briefly on the work of two figures named Stanley—the philosopher Stanley Cavell and the theologian Stanley Hauerwas. But before doing so, I should also add a word of warning. While both Cavell and Hauerwas locate marriage at the very heart of their work, their respective accounts of marriage are decidedly un-romantic. Or at least they do not have much use for the sort of self-confirming, feel-good emotions we tend to think of as romantic.

This is most bluntly reflected by Stanley Hauerwas in his account of how marriages tend to follow what he calls Hauerwas's law, which he summarizes as follows:

> we always marry the wrong person. We never know whom we marry; we just think we do. Or even if we first marry the right person, just give it a while and he or she will change. For marriage, being what it is, means we are not the same person after we have entered it. The primary problem morally is learning how to love and care for this stranger to whom you find yourself married.[1]

It is important to recognize that Hauerwas's law is structured in such a way that it is reversible. If it is true that we never really know the person to whom we get married, it follows that we always marry the right person as well. The point Hauerwas is trying to make is that marriage is less a question about finding the right partner in a world of potential candidates than it is a commitment to a certain sort of ongoing work. It

---

[1] Hauerwas, *A Community of Character*, 172.

is a project that demands the transformation of the selves who entered into it. While Hauerwas's law will no doubt sound like a downer to young couples who think their love for one another is sufficient to sustain a marriage, he insists that it is actually good news. Indeed, he argues that it reflects the sort of good news that constitutes the Christian gospel. "It suggests that it is perfectly normal for partners in a marriage to discover, in time, that each person has some trait about which the other had not bargained. . . . [O]ur culture trains us to assume that for a marriage to succeed we need to be 'right' for one another. Hauerwas's law frees us from that demanding requirement."[2] In other words, Hauerwas helps us see that marriage is an exercise in working through difference and conflict. Most significantly, it allows us to avoid the fantasy that conflict is necessarily something from which we have to emerge victorious. And it teaches us that difficulty is not always something from which we must attempt to plot an escape.

A similar view of marriage can also be found in the work of the philosopher Stanley Cavell, and in particular his understanding of the tension between acknowledgment and avoidance. One of the most interesting aspects of Cavell's work is his claim that the central questions of philosophy are the very same questions that animate the dramas of Shakespeare and the Hollywood comedies of married life, especially those of the 1930s and 40s. In both cases, Cavell argues that marriage is envisioned as a form of remarriage. "The drive of the plot" in these dramas, he suggests, "is not to get the central pair together, but to get them back together, together again."[3] They picture "the mystery of marriage by finding that neither law nor sexuality (nor, by implication, progeny), is sufficient to ensure true marriage and suggesting that what provides legitimacy is the mutual willingness for remarriage, for a sort of continuous reaffirmation."[4] The genre of the remarriage drama, he adds, is "of a sort that leads to acknowledgment; to a reconciliation of a genuine forgiveness; a reconciliation so profound as to require the metamorphosis of death and revival; the achievement of a new perspective on existence; a perspective that presents itself as a place, one removed from the city of confusion and divorce."[5] Where it is

---

[2] Hauerwas, *Hannah's Child*, 243.

[3] Cavell, *Pursuits of Happiness*, 2. See also Cavell, *Disowning Knowledge*, 18.

[4] Cavell, *Pursuits of Happiness*, 142.

[5] Ibid., 19.

appropriate to talk about happiness, whether in a marriage or in a life more generally, Cavell suggests that "[t]he achievement of happiness requires not the perennial and fuller satisfaction of our needs as they stand but the examination and transformation of those needs."[6]

Without getting into too much detail, let me remind you that Cavell's work is built around the observation that the traditional philosophical questions about the possibility of knowledge and the so-called problem of other minds have the same form as the dynamics he finds at work in the drama of marriage. In suggesting that both philosophy and marriage are structured around a tension between acknowledgement and avoidance, Cavell calls us to give up our lust for dominion and to appreciate that our lives are finite, partial, and vulnerable. He claims that good philosophy and good marriages allow us to accept our humanity, that we are constituted by flesh and blood.[7] This is to practice a form of knowledge in which the possibility of knowing ourselves is intimately bound up with knowing the existence of another, of knowing another precisely as other. Or rather, it suggests that our pursuits should be framed not so much in terms of a merely intellectual quest for knowledge as an ethical task of acknowledgement, of putting ourselves in another's presence.[8] All of this involves acknowledging our separateness just as much as it frames our desire to be together.

Now, I don't know about you. But I find these accounts of marriage far more interesting and compelling than the standard romantic vision we often associate with searching for and hopefully finding a "true love" with whom we might spend the rest of our life together in marriage. They suggest instead that true love is not so much an object we are searching for but a performance that calls for ongoing practice and extended work. A good marriage, we might say, is not something we might be lucky enough to enjoy if we are able to find and hold onto another person who is just the right fit for our unique personality. It is rather something made and remade. Of course, a marriage can only be made and remade where two people are equally committed to the difficult art of remarriage. So it's not that the question of whom we marry is entirely irrelevant. But Cavell and Hauerwas help us understand that marriages can only be made and remade to the extent that we are

---

[6] Ibid., 5.
[7] See Cavell, *Disowning Knowledge*, 136.
[8] Ibid., 104.

open to the possibility of being surprised by finding joy in something we didn't know we wanted.

Whether a drama of marriage turns out to be tragic or comedic depends upon a couple's readiness for remarriage. Comedies of remarriage are those which reflect a capacity for acknowledgement, while tragedies are those in which one or both of the partners give in to fantasies of avoidance. Cavell's vision of marriage as remarriage calls for the couple to rediscover one another and so to let the other be the other rather than violently reducing one another to some static image of the same. Marriage, in other words, is not just about two becoming one. It is also about how this one meaningfully remains two. As Cavell puts it, "this ceremony of union takes the form of a ceremony of separation, thus declaring that the question of two becoming one is just half the problem; the other half is how one becomes two."[9] Notice how similar Cavell's formula for marriage is to Hauerwas's law.

That the marriage of Harry and Agnes is appropriately described as a comedy is not only demonstrated by the fact that we have gathered together to celebrate with them today, some 50 years after their wedding in Crystal City Mennonite Church. It is also suggested by the fact that it has produced so much genuine, life-changing laughter, as I'm sure you can all relate. I have witnessed their capacity for laughter as arising from the sense in which theirs is a marriage of the sort Cavell describes, a relationship in which two become one while remaining two. Their laughter reflects their appreciation, with Hauerwas, that they are simultaneously wrong and right for one another, and that this is a beautiful thing.

By way of conclusion, let me return to the question of the program. What if the program is central to the Hildebrand family for the same reason that Cavell insists that good philosophy demands a healthy appreciation for drama and film? What if the life of the family and life in general is best understood as a sort of ongoing performance art? Then it makes all the sense in the world that we should, from time to time, find ourselves involved in programs through which we practice telling and performing our stories with one another. But it's not the program itself that matters. Rather, the program is practice for the real thing— enduring change together gracefully, learning to imagine our way into the roles we have been given and to reimagine new roles as they arise.

---

[9] Ibid., 220.

Maybe even for those, like me, who really don't enjoy them, programs provide important opportunities to practice patience and endurance. If the program can help teach us to acknowledge the unique voices of our fellow performers and let ourselves be transformed by the surprising encounter with others whose presence we could not have anticipated—those strangers we thought we knew—then perhaps the program can prepare us for the kinds of marriages and family relationships that make for comedic dramas. Thanks Mom and Dad for giving us a front row seat to just such a dramatic performance. And congratulations on 50 years of remarriage.

Chapter 16

Calling and Confessing:
What Might Dante Have to Teach Us
About Peace Sunday?

Originally preached at Charleswood Mennonite Church, Winnipeg, MB
November 13, 2016, Peace Sunday
Scripture texts: Isaiah 6: 1-8; Luke 5: 8-10

Today is the day the Mennonite church has, in its strange wisdom, come to recognize as Peace Sunday. I promise I will get there eventually. But not before embarking on a path that might at first seem like a lengthy detour that takes some surprising twists and turns. It might even seem like a way of evading the question of peace. But my hope is that it might serve as an exercise in reorientation that is consistent with the way the scripture passages we have been given today serve to reorient some ways we may be tempted to understand the significance of Peace Sunday. At the outset, let me just begin by noting that neither of our passages mentions the word peace. Rather, they are among the classic depictions of the twin themes of calling and confessing. What might this have to do with peace? Let me try to make some sense of this by taking an extended detour through of one of the greatest Christian stories ever written, Dante's *Divine Comedy*.

The *Divine Comedy* is at once the story of Dante's own life, but also and more importantly the story of our collective Christian life. He sets the stage for the story with a stark juxtaposition of two contrasting opening scenes. We might even call them two geographies or landscapes, as they are both very earthy settings. In the first opening scene, Dante tells of how he found himself in a condition of confusion and lostness, deep in the middle of a dark and shadowy forest. He describes it as a "savage forest, dense and difficult." He says that being there was almost as bitter as death itself and recalls that it left him paralyzed with fear. We learn later that the forest symbolizes the condition of sinfulness, guilt, and moral confusion.

Like a contemporary filmmaker, Dante then cuts quickly to an entirely different scene. Here he stands in an open desert field. There are no trees, and hence no shadowy darkness to obscure his vision. When he looks up, he sees that he is standing at the foot of a great mountain that reaches up toward the transcendent rays of the sun. The way up the mountain represents the way of salvation and redemption, of pilgrimage toward the Christian vision of the good life. Dante confesses to being unable to explain how he ended up wandering blindly in the forest, suggesting that it was as if he was sleepwalking his way through life. And he is equally unable to account for his arrival in the desert where he found himself looking up at the mountain. But as for what happened next, he has an awful lot to say. Three books and 100 cantos, to be exact. Unfortunately, we don't have time to explore all the fascinating details and images he manages to work in. But I think it is worth lingering for some time over the broad strokes of the story.

Alone, impatient, and eager to erase any lingering memory of the dark forest, Dante immediately sets out to climb the mountain. He is anxious to reach the summit as fast as he can and so he sets off in a straight line up toward the top. He doesn't make much progress, however, before his optimistic pace suddenly comes to a halt. His path forward is blocked by three fierce beasts—a leopard, a lion, and a she-wolf. It turns out he hasn't left the forest behind after all. For the three vicious beasts all make their home in its dark midst and they came from there to impede his attempted ascent. So Dante turns and makes his way back down the mountain. When he arrives back at the bottom, he encounters Virgil, the dead pagan poet. Virgil helps Dante understand that the three beasts symbolize the three general forms of sin—fraud, violence, and incontinence (or weakness of will). He also helps Dante to realize that he will never make it up the mountain if he tries to do so by walking in a straight line. The straight line represents the merely intellectual path which seeks to apprehend the good directly as a kind of cognitive possession. The problem with this is that it makes redemption out to be a rather straightforward matter. It depicts the way of salvation as a linear path where we can always see exactly where we are headed because it is right there in front of us. Call it the easy way.

Dante's mistake was to think he could ascend the mountain of salvation by using an approach that was not suited to the task of climbing and could only lead him back to the forest of moral confusion. This is what the encounter with the three beasts dramatizes. He thought he could think his way straight to the top. In effect, he was trying to save himself through an effort of intellectual self-sufficiency. It is significant that Dante was entirely alone both in the forest and on his first attempt up the mountain. But the mere presence of Virgil as a companion suggests that pilgrimage is not something to be attempted alone. It requires the company of others we typically call friendship. Virgil appears a friend who helps to correct the distortion of Dante's prideful and arrogant assumption that he could make his own way up the mountain through an exercise of solitary reason. To put it in terms of the medieval categories that Dante inherited and deployed, Virgil helps him to appreciate that his failure was the result of a fracture by which the necessary relationship between the faculties of intellect and will had been broken apart. The intellect might be capable of identifying and conceiving the good, just as Dante could see the sun's rays illuminating the top of the mountain. But it is the will that moves us, whether in a direction toward the good or away from it. So as long as the will is not in conformity with the intellectual conception of the good, progress toward the good is simply not possible. In the words of one recent commentator, "Dante sees the light of transcendence at the top of the mountain, yet he cannot proceed toward it insofar as his will suffers impediments."[1]

Virgil comes to Dante's aid by showing him that he must take another path, one that takes a very different form than the path on which he initially set out. Call it the path of confession and moral conversion. Conversion is a turning around, a reorientation of the self. It is a confessional change of direction away from the temptation of prideful self-sufficiency and toward humility. It involves the unmaking and refashioning of the self, a project that depends crucially on the ability to acknowledge one's vulnerable dependence on others. And so begins the journey that occupies the rest of the *Divine Comedy*. The most striking thing about Dante's journey is that after the opening juxtaposition of the forest and mountain scenes, his movement never follows any straight lines. Having been saved from his foolish attempt to pursue the straight way up the mountain, Virgil leads Dante on a curved path that is always turning and winding around. Moreover, it does not initially

---

[1] Harrison, *Forests*, 83.

proceed by going up. Rather, it begins by heading in a downward direction. Under the guidance of Virgil, Dante descends into the depths of hell to encounter those whose lives were distorted by sin in its various forms. It is only by a serious confessional reckoning that is capable of seeing sin for what it really is—the prideful separation of the self from God, the giver of life—that the soul is prepared for the work of what we might call moral education.

Virgil thus leads Dante on a winding path that spirals down through the various levels of hell. Each successive level is a step further removed from God and brings Dante into contact with those whose lives have turned in on themselves. At the end of this humbling and harrowing confessional journey Dante re-emerges and finds himself once again at the foot of the very same mountain he originally encountered when he found himself inexplicably on the outside of the forest. It is worth noting that the base of the mountain is reached only by proceeding all the way down and piercing through the very floor of hell before emerging on the other side. From the perspective of the world, we can only head down through the darkness of hell before we are given an opportunity for new life on the far side of the world. At this point we do well to remember that the Greek word for church, *ekklēsia*, literally means to be called out from the world—*klēsis* being the Greek word for "call" and *ek* the prefix that means "out" or "from" like the English prefix "ex." Echoing the story of the church, Dante's initial "worldly" perspective is literally inverted or overturned. Virgil's winding path doesn't just turn Dante around. It also turns him upside-down and finds him being taken entirely outside of the world he originally knew. Or rather, we might say that Dante has been turned right-side up. It is only after he emerges from his journey through hell that he is set down properly with his feet on the ground. It was his initial vision of linear intellectual ascent that was wrongheaded and hence upside-down.

On Dante's second encounter with the mountain, the landscape is not that of a barren desert slope from which he originally approached. Rather, we are presented with a scenery that is draped with rich, fertile swaths of various sorts of botanical life and so is bathed in the hopeful colour of green. This suggests another important resonance associated with the image of turning that comes into clearer focus as Dante returns to the mountain this second time around—the turning of the soil we call cultivation, which is necessary for growth. The mountain is now known as the mountain of purgatory and its ascent depicts the process of moral formation. As Virgil and Dante undertake their spiraling journey up the mountain, they encounter the souls of those whose lives have been shaped by vices we know as the seven deadly sins. Through these encounters, Dante experiences a turning of the soul as it is cultivated and prepared for new moral growth. The movement through purgatory stages a story of conversion, whereby Dante's distorted will is refashioned and the marks of the seven sins are ultimately erased from his forehead. As the weight of each successive sin is lifted, he becomes increasingly lighter, making it easier for him to move up the mountain. The process of cultivation whereby the vices are turned and transformed into virtues is only finally completed in paradise, which is itself depicted as the perpetual turning of the planets in a kind of cosmic harmony like a spinning wheel. But let us stick with this striking image of moral conversion as a form of gardening that is suggested by one final crucial scene at the top of mount purgatory.

Here Dante finds himself once again in a forest, or rather a garden— the Garden of Eden, which we are also to understand as a vision of earthly paradise. It is also at this point that Virgil must take leave of Dante and gives him over to Beatrice. It finally becomes clear that it is Beatrice who sent Virgil to rescue Dante from himself. Among other things, Beatrice represents the biblical and Christian theme of calling. Just as God first calls Israel and then that new form of community we call church, so Beatrice is a messenger through whom God called Dante. At the risk of oversimplification, we might say that Dante is doubly called. He is called out from the forest of moral confusion. And he is also called out from the foolish thought that the good life can be achieved by the straight way of intellectual ascent. In this respect, the opening two scenes represent different forms of worldly sinfulness out of which Beatrice calls Dante and, by extension, God calls the church. But more than anything else, the *Divine Comedy* demonstrates, in a richly dramatic way, that the call of God is only capable of being heard by those who are capable of confession and conversion, those whose souls have been turned away from arrogance and pride and toward humble gift of love with which God first called us.

It is this close relationship between calling, confession, and conversion that is reflected in the passages from Isaiah and Luke. Isaiah is called by way of the seraphs. But how does he respond? He responds by saying "Woe is me! I am lost, for I am a man of unclean lips, and I live among a people of unclean lips." And yet, he continues, "my eyes have seen the King, the Lord of hosts." (Isa. 6:5) Notice how much this sounds like the opening scenes of the Divine Comedy. Merely to see the Lord intellectually, as Isaiah does, is one thing. But we can only truly see when our will has been brought into conformity with that vision through a process of moral conversion. In Isaiah this is achieved by a burning piece of coal that is touched to his lips. In Dante, it is achieved through a twisting journey through hell and back up mount purgatory. But the main point is the same. Call and conversion exist in a kind of mutual, dialectical relationship with one another.

The passage from Luke takes up this same dynamic as if from the other side. When Simon Peter sees Jesus, he falls down at Jesus's knees and confesses that he is but a sinful man. Jesus responds not only by calling him as a disciple, but also by giving over this same task of calling disciples to Simon Peter. As one who has confessed his sinfulness, he is now worthy to go fishing for people. Unlike those arrogant souls who take it upon themselves to call people to the way of Jesus, we find that Jesus himself chooses those who have humbly turned themselves around and upside-down in a form of confession that acknowledges their unworthiness.

Now, what might any of this have to do with Peace Sunday? I cannot help but think that these passages serve to counter the temptation to assume an arrogant attitude toward peace. I suspect Mennonites may be tempted to feel a certain sort of triumphalism on Peace Sunday. A quiet, self-effacing sort of triumphalism, to be sure. But a triumphalism nonetheless. We might be tempted to think that we have got this peace thing figured out and that our task is to share this special insight with a world full of others who remain mired in various sorts of confused violence. To put it in Dante's terms, we often map our discourse of peace onto something like the straight way, the merely intellectual way. This happens, for example, when we speak of peace as an ideal and see ourselves as those whose task is to work toward it in a sort of linear fashion. But that is not the logic of the passages of Scripture we have been given today. Nor is it the logic of the *Divine Comedy*, which dramatizes the twin themes of call and confession in such a powerful and compelling way. The point of reading these passages in the context of Peace Sunday seems to be that if there is a path to peace, it is not the straight way. Rather, it is the curved way of confession that gets turned around and upside-down as it takes a longer, more circuitous, and more arduous path. This is a path that first descends and turns decisively upon our ability to cultivate an ability to see how we remain implicated in various forms of self-deceptive violence. Perhaps, like Isaiah, we need to have our lips burned so that we can speak words of peace more truthfully.

There is no question that the world could do well to hear a clear word or two about peace. But it most certainly doesn't need any more easy speech about peace. Rather, we are called, with Dante, to the humble speech of confession and conversion. Like soil at the hands of gardeners, we are called to have our violent souls turned over in the ongoing work of confession and conversion so that we might be able to nourish more peaceable forms of life. Whether that gets heard by others is not finally our problem. Our task is to be faithful to the call of God that keeps coming to us in spite of our inability to hear it, whether through seraphs, new versions of Beatrice, or some other as yet unrecognizable source that might be more akin to the pagan Virgil who was sent to rescue Dante. We may be called to be peacemakers and we may even claim to have a vision of what the peace of Christ looks like. But that is all too often understood in merely intellectual terms which neglects the need to cultivate the will. We exist not in the earthly paradise of the Garden of Eden, let alone the celestial paradise in which we see God face to face. And yet hopefully we are at least located somewhere on the winding, confessional path of pilgrimage and not foolishly attempting to undertake another straight ascent up the mountain. For there is no more sure way to guarantee that we will fall back down into the forest of darkness and violence than to set out on a straight path for peace.

Bibliography

Badiou, Alain. *St Paul: The Foundation of Universalism*. Stanford, CA: Stanford University Press, 2003.

Barth, Karl. *The Word of God and the Word of Man*. Translated by Douglas Horton. New York, NY: Harper Torchbooks, 1957.

Bossy, John. *Christianity in the West: 1400-1700*. Oxford: Oxford University Press, 1985.

Cavell, Stanley. *Disowning Knowledge in Seven Plays of Shakespeare*. Updated Edition. Cambridge: Cambridge University Press, 2003.

Cavell, Stanley. *Little Did I Know: Excerpts from Memory*. Stanford, CA: Stanford University Press, 2010.

Cavell, Stanley. *Pursuits of Happiness: The Hollywood Comedy of Remarriage*. Cambridge, MA: Harvard University Press, 1981.

Dante. *Paradiso*. Translated by Robert Hollander and Jean Hollander. New York, NY: Anchor Books, 2007.

Dante, *Purgatorio*. Translated by Robert Hollander and Jean Hollander. New York, NY: Anchor Books, 2003.

Deleuze, Gilles. *Kafka: Toward a Minor Literature*. Translated by Dana Polan. Minneapolis, MN: University of Minnesota Press, 1986.

Dula, Peter. *Cavell, Companionship, and Christian Theology*. Oxford: Oxford University Press, 2011.

Freccero, John. *Dante: The Poetics of Conversion*. Harvard, MA: Harvard University Press, 1986.

Griffiths, Paul J. *The Vice of Curiosity: An Essay on Intellectual Appetite*. Winnipeg, MB: CMU Press, 2006.

Harrison, Robert. *Forests: The Shadow of Civilization*. Chicago, IL: University of Chicago Press, 1992.

Hauerwas, Stanley. *A Community of Character: Toward a Constructive Christian Social Ethic*. Notre Dame, IN: University of Notre Dame Press, 1981.

Hauerwas, Stanley. "Christianity: It's Not a Religion, It's an Adventure." In *The Hauerwas Reader*. Edited by John Berkman and Michael Cartwright. Durham, NC: Duke University Press, 2001.

Hauerwas, Stanley. *Hannah's Child: A Theologian's Memoir*. Grand Rapids, MI: Eerdmans, 2010.

Hauerwas, Stanley. *Working with Words: On Learning to Speak Christian*. Eugene, OR: Cascade Books, 2011.

Hrosvit of Gandersheim. "The Martyrdom of the Holy Virgins Fides, Spes, and Karitas (*Sapientia*)." In *The Plays of Hrotsvit of Gandersheim*. Translated by Katharina Wilson. New York, NY: Garland Publishing, Inc., 1989.

Huebner, Chris K. *A Precarious Peace: Yoderian Explorations on Theology Knowledge, and Identity*. Scottdale, PA: Herald Press, 2006.

Johnson, Elizabeth. *She Who Is: The Mystery of God in Feminist Theological Discourse*. Tenth Anniversary Edition. New York, NY: Herder & Herder, 2002.

McCabe, Herbert. *God Matters*. Springfield, IL: Templegate Publishers, 1987.

Moevs, Christian. *The Metaphysics of Dante's* Comedy. Oxford: Oxford University Press, 2005.

Rendell, Matt. *The Death of Marco Pantani*. London: Weidenfeld & Nicolson, 2006.

Robinson, Marilynne. *Gilead*. New York, NY: Farrar, Strauss and Giroux, 2004.

Robinson, Marilynne. *Housekeeping*. New York, NY: Farrar, Strauss and Giroux, 1980.

Williams, Rowan. *A Ray of Darkness: Sermons and Reflections*. Boston, MA: Cowley Publications, 1995.

Williams, Rowan. *Christ on Trial: How the Gospel Unsettles Our Judgement.* Grand Rapids, MI: Eerdmans, 2000.

Williams, Rowan. "Theological Integrity." Chap. in *On Christian Theology.* Oxford: Blackwell, 2000.

Williams, Rowan. *The Wound of Knowledge: A Theological History from the New Testament to Luther and St. John of the Cross.* Reprint Edition. Eugene, OR: Wipf and Stock Publishers, 1998.

Wolin, Sheldon. *Politics and Vision: Continuity and Innovation in Western Political Thought.* Princeton, NJ: Princeton University Press, 2004.